POEMS
AND
SONGS
OF
ROBERT BURNS

Nancy Marshall

Chambers

CHAMBERS
An imprint of Larousse plc
43–45 Annandale Street
Edinburgh EH7 4AZ

First published by Chambers 1991
Reprinted 1994

A CIP catalogue record for this book is
available from the British Library

ISBN 0 550 20068 1

Illustrations by G. W. Lennox Paterson and John Marshall
© Larousse plc
Cover design by John Marshall

Typeset by Pillans & Wilson Ltd, Edinburgh and London
Printed in Singapore by
Singapore National Printers Ltd

Contents

The Life of Robert Burns   1

Poems and Songs
Address to the Deil   17
Address to the Unco Guid, or the
    Rigidly Righteous   23
Ae Fond Kiss   26
Afton Water   28
A Red, Red Rose   30
Auld Lang Syne   32
Bruce to his Men at Bannockburn   34
Coming through the Rye   36
Death and Dr Hornbook   37
A Man's a Man for a' that   44
Holy Willie's Prayer   46
John Anderson, my Jo   51
Lines written on the Window of a Room
    in Stirling   52
John Barleycorn   53
My Bonie Mary   56
O whistle, and I'll come to you, my Lad   58
Poor Mailie's Elegy   60
Tam o' Shanter   62
The Auld Farmer's New-Year Morning
    Salutation to his Auld Mare, Maggie   70
The Banks o' Doon   74
The Cotter's Saturday Night   76
The Deil's awa wi' th' Exciseman   83
The Holy Fair   85
The Last Time I came o'er the Moor   93
The Rigs o' Barley   95
The Selkirk Grace   97
The Twa Dogs   98
To a Mouse   107
To Dr Blacklock   109
Willie brew'd a Peck o' Maut   113
Willie Wastle   114

The Burns Supper   119
To a Haggis   119

Bibliography   123

Index of First Lines   124

The Life of Robert Burns

Robert Burns lived and died during the last half of the eighteenth century. A century which saw the Union of the Crowns, the failure of two Jacobite rebellions and the savage atrocities committed against Burns's own countrymen by 'Butcher Cumberland' (1721–65), the second son of George II, on behalf of the English crown. This Ayrshire ploughman, writing in vernacular Scots, filled a need in a nation seeing its national identity engulfed by an ever-encroaching Englishness.

Trying to unravel the true nature of Robert Burns seems impossible, full of contradictions and as fickle as the Scottish weather. Warm and witty, suspicious and sarcastic, he was a hardworking farmer, drinker and womanizer, poet and lyric writer, as well as a Jacobite sympathizer with republican leanings.

A rigorous early life spent labouring on his father's farm took its toll both physically and mentally. The constant threat of eviction for non-payment of rent left Robert Burns with a life-long insecurity, which perhaps accounts for his violent personality changes. Over the years he has been sentimentalized and his more bawdy works altered or suppressed, including some he never intended to publish. The tales of his female conquests are mostly true, few friendships remained platonic. In his youth he maintained that love itself moved him to write, but his satires and supernatural tales prove it was more than fancy that stirred him.

By the time of his death in 1796, he was worn out, physically ill with a recurring heart condition and fearful for his family's future. He was little more than a shadow of the vigorous 'ploughman poet', who had conquered Edinburgh only nine years previously. True, he had been forced to expend a great deal of energy, in those nine years, initially combining the work of Ellisland farm with the duties of an excise officer, which meant covering 200 miles a week on horseback. At this very same time he was writing, altering and compiling almost 400 songs for two different collections. Notwithstanding this enormous effort, he managed to produce work of such enduring sentiment, that today, two centuries later, it still has the power to lift the spirits.

With regard to the poet's early life, his father William Burnes settled in Ayrshire in 1750, but hailed originally from Kincardineshire, in the north-east of Scotland. His family had been tenant farmers of the estate of Earl Marischal, a staunch Stuart supporter. In later life, the romantic in Robert liked to believe that his ancestors' fall on hard times was due to their loyalty to the Jacobite cause, rather than such mundane reasons as his grandfather's over ambitious farming ventures or a succession of bad harvests. Whatever the reasons, the Burnes's household was broken up in 1748 due to bankruptcy and the sons William and Robert went elsewhere in search of work. The poet's father, William, walked to Edinburgh and found work as a gardener, being employed for a time in helping to lay out 'the Meadows'.

In 1750 he moved to Ayrshire on the west coast of Scotland, where he continued as a gardener, first for the Laird of Fairlee, then with the Crawfords of Doonside and finally at Doonholm for Dr Fergusson. During this time, this determined, hardworking man put aside enough money to lease seven and a half acres of land in Alloway, where he planned to build a house and set up as a market gardener. He continued working at Doonholm while he began his market garden. In 1757, just seven years after his arrival in Ayrshire, during the summer and autumn he built, with his own hands, the 'auld clay biggin', known all over the world today as Burns's Cottage. It was built as a home for his bride Agnes Brown, the daughter of an Ayrshire tenant farmer, whom he married on 15 December that year. By then William Burnes was thirty-six years of age and his new wife twenty-five. He was a slim, wiry figure of medium height and she was a small, vivacious red-head. They both possessed strong tempers, both had the ethos of hard work stamped through them and probably because of their 'late' marriage, both brought maturity and stability to a relationship which survived happily until William's death in 1784. Robert, the first of their seven children, was born on 25 January 1759.

In Alloway the family's life passed pleasantly. While William Burnes continued to work as a gardener and run his small market garden, his wife looked after the dairy, and along with her cousin Betty Davidson, entertained the children with old Scottish songs and tall tales, which, unknown to them, were to stimulate Burns's imagination and influence his work all his days. In 1765, at the age of six, and with his younger brother Gilbert, Robert entered the village school of Alloway for his first formal education. Sadly, after little more than a month, the schoolmaster left for Ayr and the school closed. An ever-resourceful William Burnes quickly got together with the heads of four other families and found a new master for the school, arranging that they split the cost of his salary between them and take it in turns to board him.

John Murdoch, the young man who filled the post, regarded Robert and Gilbert as bright and hardworking; Gilbert, of the two, he thought had a 'more lively imagination' and was 'more of a wit, than Robert', and musically he found 'Robert's ear, in particular, was remarkably dull, and his voice untunable.' Murdoch continued to teach the boys for a time, although only sporadically, after the family moved to Mount Oliphant farm early in 1766. By then, William Burnes thought the cottage too small for his growing family and to prevent his children becoming labourers and therefore 'underlings' in another household, he leased Mount Oliphant, a few miles from Alloway, at forty pounds per year, becoming a tenant farmer like his ancestors. And he was to fare no better. In these seventy acres of exhausted soil, which hardly covered the rocks beneath, the family toiled in backbreaking work and lived in extreme frugality for the next twelve years. During that time Robert performed a man's work, when he was still little more than a child, and in the process irreversibly damaged his heart.

He described his time there as being 'the cheerless gloom of a hermit, with the unceasing moil of a galley slave'. Gilbert believed that Robert's later melancholia and the depressions which haunted him all his adult life stemmed from this time. Describing Robert's physical condition he said, 'At this time he was almost constantly afflicted in the evenings with a dull headache, which, at a subsequent period of his life, was exchanged for a palpitation of the heart, and a threatening of fainting and suffocation in the night time.' Robert's drastic measures to stop the palpitations included keeping a bucket of water at his bedside into which he stuck his head in the hope of relieving the spasm.

During these years William Burnes, when not teaching Robert and Gilbert himself, and instructing them on the Bible, periodically sent them to different schools to brush up on their work. It shows the remarkable strength and character of this kindly, but stern father, that even while trying to eke out an existence for the family and contend with threatening letters from the factor (an agent who managed estates of others) over unpaid rent, he still found the time and inclination to foster the future for his children.

By the age of eighteen, Robert, a compulsive reader from his earliest days, had devoured the works of Shakespeare, Milton, Dryden, Gray, Shenstone, Pope and Addison. Apart from the fiction of Henry Fielding and Tobias Smollett and the philosophy and history of David Hume and William Robertson, he knew intimately the works of his predecessors in Scottish literature, Allan Ramsay and Robert Fergusson, he read French and had a little Latin. The Bible, as he was to depict in 'The Cotter's Saturday Night', was standard reading for any God-fearing Scottish family. Hardly the background of an 'unlettered ploughman'.

In 1777 Robert's horizons widened immeasurably when his father decided to take the lease of

Lochlie farm, three miles from Mauchline and two and a half miles from Tarbolton. In farming terms, it was little better a bargain than Mount Oliphant, either financially (the rent was high at one pound per acre for each of the 130 acres) or in soil condition. William Burnes had merely exchanged poor exhausted soil for swampy, undrained land, but for the next four years his family enjoyed a more comfortable lifestyle and Robert found new friends and stimulating company in the nearby farms and villages.

In 1780 the Tarbolton Bachelors' Club was founded and Robert became one of its leading lights, delighting in the debates and gaining confidence from the fierce interchange of passions and personalities. By the following year the poet had become a freemason in St David's Lodge, Tarbolton and it was due to this early masonic commitment that Burns found his later entry into Edinburgh made easier. The ladies had by then also begun to interest him. In his earlier youth, the charms of Nellie Kirkpatrick and Peggy Thomson had disturbed him and now at twenty-two he developed an attachment to Alison Begbie, a farmer's daughter. She turned down his offer of marriage and, depressed and dejected, Burns went off to Irvine to learn the art of flax dressing. He did set up in business with a partner, but the venture failed. His great friend from the Irvine days was Richard Brown, a sailor and great ladies' man, who, if the stories are to be believed, led Burns astray with his libidinous attitude to women. But, more importantly, he was the first person to suggest that Robert become a poet.

On his return to Lochlie early in 1782, Burns found his father involved in litigation with the factor over arrears in rent. The weather had been bad and consequently the harvests poor, and this, combined with a general downturn in the economy, toppled many small Ayrshire farmers of that period. By the time the sheriff's officers came to the farm to sell their cattle, tools and crops on 17 May 1783, William Burnes was ill with consumption and physically frail after all his years of hard labour. It is not surprising that Robert developed such an acute hatred of the landowning classes after years of watching his father being tormented by their factors making demands for money he could not find; this final sequestration of all their goods and chattels strengthened Robert's belief that all men should share the same rights and privileges. William Burnes died at Lochlie on 17 February 1784 and was buried in Alloway Kirkyard, the scene of Tam o' Shanter's nightmare encounter with the witches.

Burns's spirit was perhaps embittered by life's inequalities, but his brain was as sharp as ever, and in the previous autumn of 1783, some five months before his father's death, he and Gilbert arranged to rent Mossgiel farm to provide, as Gilbert later described it, 'an asylum for the family in case of the worst'. They also shrewdly claimed against their father's bankrupt estate as employees, and with this money and whatever savings the family had, after William Burnes's death, removed to Mossgiel, where Robert became head of the family. It was at this point that the 'e' was dropped from their surname. Mossgiel, a 118-acre property, with an annual rent of ninety pounds, lay one mile from Mauchline, and with its heavy clay soil and high elevation it was to prove no better a bargain than the previous farms, even though Robert, determined to make it a success, voraciously read agriculture books, attended markets and searched to find the best seed. However, the combination of a new-found independence and responsibility as head of the family, seemed to release in him an enormous creative force. True, he had begun his First Commonplace Book at Lochlie, in which he jotted down ideas, thoughts and impressions about life, while he continued to write both poetry and prose, but here at Mossgiel between the years of 1784 and 1786, he produced work of such exceptional calibre that, had he never written another word, he would still have been recognized as a great poet.

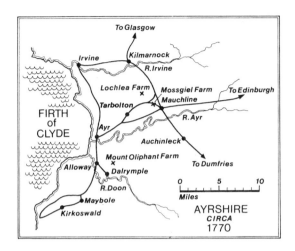

The ecclesiastical satires 'Holy Willie's Prayer', 'Address to the Deil' and 'The Holy Fair', come from this time, as do 'The Twa Dogs', 'To a Mouse', 'The Jolly Beggars', 'The Cotter's Saturday Night' and 'Address to the Unco Guid'.

But apart from this prolific output and the strain of working the farm, Robert also found time for new and influential friends like his landlord Gavin Hamilton and the lawyer Robert Aiken of Ayr. John Richmond, one of Gavin Hamilton's clerks and James Smith, a local draper, together with Burns made up a well-known trio in Mauchline, enjoying many evenings in the Whiteford Inn or Poosie Nansie's hostelry. His reputation as a poet was well known locally, but his fame was spreading too amongst 'The Belles of Mauchline'. In May 1785, his first illegitimate child, a daughter, named Elizabeth, was born to Betty Paton, one of the servants on the farm, and by the end of the same year he had wooed and won Jean Armour: their first set of twins was born the following September. Both these events brought down the wrath of the Kirk Session of Mauchline Parish Church on the poet's head: he had to appear publicly in church to be condemned for the sin of fornication.

This was common practice in Scotland at that time, but for Burns it was bitter humiliation, especially in the case of Jean Armour. After his initial delight at her pregnancy and his written promise of marriage (then recognized as a legal and binding contract) he was shattered to find that Jean's father, totally opposed to the match; had taken steps to have both of their names cut out of the document. His anger and bitterness were reserved for Jean, disgusted by her weakness in handing over the paper to her father; from his viewpoint she had committed an act of betrayal. Jean Armour did become his wife in April 1788 and it was those very qualities of passivity and acceptance, which he had despised in her, that gave him so much licence before and after their marriage. But James Armour, master mason and respected citizen of Mauchline was not yet finished with the local rhyming rake. In the early summer of 1786, in the knowledge that Burns was in the process of publishing what is now known as the Kilmarnock edition of his poems, he determined to have a financial settlement for Jean and had a warrant issued against the poet for a substantial sum of money. But wily Burns had calculated his actions and had already signed his share of Mossgiel over to Gilbert, ostensibly for the support of Betty Paton's child and included 'the profits that may arise from the publication of my poems presently in the press'.

Burns continued to agonize over Jean and what he saw as her appalling treatment of him, but true to form, in the middle of this turmoil, he turned to Mary Campbell, better known today as 'Highland Mary', and in May of that year proceeded to offer her marriage, while thinking about emigrating to Jamaica, to work as a bookkeeper. Whether he was planning to take Mary with him is a matter of conjecture, as is the manner of her death in October of that same year. It was said to be caused by typhus or possibly childbed fever, but there is no certain evidence.

On 31 July 1786 the Kilmarnock edition of his work was published and in one month the total 612 copies were sold out. Public response was deafening, his poems were read from cottage to castle. The literary world was stunned by the extraordinary talent of this supposed 'unlettered ploughman'. On 3 September Jean Armour gave birth to twins, a boy and girl. Burns left Mossgiel on 27 November for what was to be the first of two winters spent in Edinburgh. We must remember that he did not arrive in Edinburgh either friendless, socially inept or intellectually inferior. John Richmond, his friend from Mauchline now lived there, his masonic affiliations brought many useful contacts, the *literati* fêted him after their 'master' Henry Mackenzie's applause and 'society' drooled over him when the Earl of Glencairn give his seal of approval. His dress was restrained, his conversation sharp, satirical and decisive, his wit unmatched. His instincts fortunately overruled the often proffered advice to tone down the Scots in his work and while there is no doubt that he thoroughly enjoyed the fuss he created, in the midst of the social whirl, this well-educated, well-read ploughman, with his feet firmly on the ground, never lost sight of his novelty value. He described his situation in a letter to a friend:

'When proud fortune's ebbing tide recedes' – you may bear me witness, when my bubble of fame was at the highest, I stood, unintoxicated, with the inebriating cup in my hand, looking forward, with rueful resolve, to the hastening time when the stroke of envious Calumny, with all the eagerness of vengeful triumph, should dash it to the ground.

On the other hand, Edinburgh did provide him with convivial company such as the Crochallan Fencibles, a drinking club of lawyers and merchants, who met regularly at a tavern in Anchor Place. It was here that Burns met Alexander Cunningham, an Edinburgh lawyer, who proved a good and loyal friend to him during his lifetime and a great support to Jean Armour after her husband's death. Connections he made in the capital also helped to further his ambition of becoming an excise officer and Patrick Miller, a banker in the city, offered him the lease on Ellisland farm in Dumfriesshire. Most importantly he saw a second edition of his poems published, a run of some 3000, on 21 April 1787 by William Creech. A notorious skinflint, Creech cunningly bought the copyright for a hundred guineas and managed to hold back payment for sales and subscriptions for another two years. Burns turned down the offer of Ellisland farm, although he did visit there during his tour of the Borders in May of that year. At this point in his life he saw a return to farming as a regressive step back into backbreaking toil and poverty; he therefore pushed for an excise position, enlisting all the influence he could muster, while friends assured him that a ploughman he was and a ploughman he should stay.

During the rest of 1787 Burns travelled quite extensively through Scotland. Apart from his Borders tour, in June he travelled to Argyll, to the west Highlands and in August he began a three-week journey around the Highlands with his friend William Nicol, staying with the Duke and Duchess of Atholl at Blair Castle, dining at Castle Gordon at Fochabers, visiting Culloden Moor, the scene of the last Jacobite stand and the site of the Battle of Bannockburn. In October, in the company of Dr James Adair, Burns travelled through Stirling on the way to Harvieston in Clackmannanshire to stay with the Chalmers family. The Chalmers were relatives of Gavin Hamilton. Burns had met and admired their daughter Peggy before and he now proposed marriage to her, but was turned down.

Meanwhile in July of that same year between his travels, he had returned to Mossgiel and found James Armour with an entirely different view of him. Now that the father of Jean's twins was a famous, celebrated and, he assumed, soon to be wealthy poet, he was a decidedly different catch from the unsuccessful farmer and local scribbler Jean's father had previously refused. Still bitter about her, Burns reluctantly visited Jean and their children and by the following March she had produced their second set of twins. Sadly, both children died within a few weeks of their birth.

The 'Clarinda' (or Mrs Agnes McLehose) episode from December 1787 until the following spring is a curious hiatus in Burns's life; apart from the, now famous, passionate correspondence between them and the beautiful love song 'Ae Fond Kiss', it appears to have suspended him from reality for a time.

Burns signed the lease on Ellisland farm in Dumfriesshire on 18 March 1788 and by the end of April he and Jean Armour were married by mutual declaration. He still pursued an excise post as a safeguard against the failure of the farm and in July he was issued with a commission, although he did not receive an appointment until September 1789. With it came a salary of fifty pounds per annum. In June he moved to Ellisland to organize the building of a farmhouse, Jean remaining at Mauchline with their only son, his twin sister having died the previous year. They joined Burns at Christmas, living in a cottage until the farmhouse was finally finished the following summer. Ellisland stands beside the River Nith, six miles north of the town of Dumfries and with its exhausted, undrained, unfertilized soil and a rent of seventy pounds per year, it was certainly a poor investment. However, for the next three years Burns lived there with Jean and their growing brood of children, combining the arduous toil of working an unproductive farm with his excise post. It was with great relief that he managed to extricate himself from the Ellisland lease and in November 1791 the family moved into a flat in Stinking Vennel ('vennel' – lane) in Dumfries, remaining there until May 1793, when they found a red sandstone house in Mill Vennel (now Burns Street) where the poet died three years later. In Dumfries Burns concentrated his efforts on his excise work and despite his outbursts of republican sympathy for the French Revolution, he was a valued officer, often commended and subsequently promoted.

During the Dumfriesshire years, in spite of the workload, ill-health and the cares of a growing family, Burns never lost his eye for the 'fairer sex'. Anne Park, the barmaid at the Globe Inn in Dumfries, produced his daughter in March 1791, after which Jean, in her usual docile way, took the child into her home and brought her up as one of her own. Jean Lorimer, the daughter of a local farmer, inspired his 'Chloris' songs and the beautiful and bright Maria Riddell filled a void in his life both intellectually and emotionally. He continued to correspond with Mrs Dunlop of Dunlop, a motherly figure, who began writing to him after reading the Kilmarnock volume of his poems. His relations with these last two ladies were unfortunately marred for a time because of his headstrong behaviour. In Maria Riddell's case the cause of the breach was the so-called 'rape of the Sabine women' incident (see 'The Last Time I came o'er The Moor') and he bitterly offended Mrs Dunlop, knowing two of her daughters were married to exiled French royalists, when he described Louis XVI and Marie Antoinette as 'a perjured blockhead and an unprincipled prostitute'. Maria Riddell regretted their estrangement and it was she who instigated the truce between them, but the divide that separated Burns and Mrs Dunlop was only mended on his death-bed, when he finally received a reply to his contrite letters. Agnes McLehose briefly entered his life once more in 1791, when she contacted him to ask for help for a servant girl, who had given birth to his son after he left Edinburgh. And only a few months before his death he was writing tributes to his nurse Jessie Lewars, the sister of a fellow excise officer. Jean Armour bore him nine children, made him a home and tolerated his extra-marital activities, in the knowledge that she would rather live with him than live without him. Burns loved his children deeply and was always concerned for their future welfare. Jean he loved in his own way, but she could share only part of his life, that of hearth and home, while he needed stimulus, both socially and intellectually to help absorb the energies of his boiling brain.

In later life Burns's artistic talents were devoted almost exclusively to Scottish song, saving many lyrics and melodies that would otherwise have been lost for ever. From 1788 until 1792 he wrote, rearranged and compiled songs for James Johnson's *Scots Musical Museum,* later performing the same task from 1792 until his death in 1796 for George Thomson's *Select Scottish Airs.* The debt we owe to him for this service is immeasurable, considering his other responsibilities, his poor health and the fact that the work was totally unpaid.

Burns's health, dogged throughout his life by depressions, melancholia and a heart condition, took a severe downturn in the last six months of his life. In addition to these old agues, he developed joint pains and 'rheumatic' fevers. He did not die from alcoholism, as has often been suggested. His doctor misdiagnosed his final illness as 'flying gout' and undoubtedly hastened his end by sending him to bathe in the freezing waters of the Solway Firth.

Unable to work in the last months, he was seriously worried about his finances and his family's future welfare, if he died. Acute shortages of food during the winter of 1795–6 caused hardship all over the country and by February and March there were riots in the streets of Dumfries. Having managed to live within his income during his lifetime, it must have hurt his pride that in the final weeks he was reduced to asking friends to repay money he had loaned and to beg others for financial assistance to pay small accounts.

His fears for Jean and the children proved unfounded due to the unstinting work of his friends Alexander Cunningham and John Syme. The collected a substantial sum of money through public subscription and from the sales of his work to ensure a comfortable and secure lifestyle for the family. Robert Burns died, aged thirty-seven, on 21 July 1796, and was buried on 25 July in St Michael's Churchyard, Dumfries. Jean, absent

13

from the funeral, as she was giving birth to their youngest child, outlived him by thirty-eight years, dying in 1834 at the age of sixty-seven.

We will probably never fully appreciate Burns's contribution to Scottish literature and to Scotland. In a nation feeling its roots slipping away, he kept the flame of patriotism burning. He translated into poetry the certainties of life in their simplest terms, good and bad, and made a celebration of them and of the experience. In less able hands the sentimentalism in his work would appear facile, but Burns was not a 'heaven-taught ploughman', but an educated and skilled craftsman in the arts of poetry and song.

Robert Burns was no stranger to the gloomier side of man's estate, having many periods of black despair, but in the midst of his pain he recognized that there were always moments, no matter how fleeting, when the spirits were lifted, the mind reassured. In his finest work he catches these moments and shares them with us. His words have the power to touch the heart and linger long after the touching.

POEMS AND SONGS

Address to the Deil

When Burns's father died in the spring of 1784 responsibility for the family fell to Robert. They moved to the farm at Mossgiel where Robert would compose his poems as he laboured behind the plough during the day, then commit them to paper in the evening darkness of the garret he shared with his brother Gilbert. The death of his father and the unrelenting toil seem to have released a font of creativity, which during the following two years produced many of Burns's most powerful works. During that first winter 1784–5 'Holy Willie's Prayer', 'The Holy Fair' and 'Address to the Deil', his three great satires against the Church, were written. The source of these glittering works lay in Burns's genius, his love of life and the village of Mauchline.

In those days Mauchline was a busy, thriving village of 1000 inhabitants with as many again in the surrounding district. As the crossroads of the Ayr-Edinburgh and Dumfries-Kilmarnock roads, it was a popular stopping off place for travellers and hosted thirteen livestock fairs and even a race day each year. It was here that the poet found friends in his landlord Gavin Hamilton and the farmer John Rankine, whose daughter Annie inspired 'Corn Rigs'.

Behind the image of Mauchline as a pleasant, bustling village, however, lay the world of the 'Holy Willies', self-appointed upholders of the strict Calvinist ideals of the time. To an intelligent man such as Burns the central tenet of Calvinism, that an 'elect' or chosen were bound for heaven whatever their actions and that the rest of mankind, no matter how well behaved could look forward only to hell fire, seemed ludicrous. This concept of predestination was reinforced by fearsome litanies from the pulpit reassuring the simple-minded congregation of the existence, shape and general moral degeneracy of 'Satan' who would surely lay hands on all of them sooner or later. Needless to say native superstition thrived on this diet of religious hokum and the devil was

17

seen at work in a howling wind, a twisted shadow or if the milk did not turn to butter in the churn.

Burns fell more directly foul of the Kirk authorities by his actions on the odd occasions when he set out to enjoy himself in Mauchline's haunts of rest and relaxation. His exploits in the Whiteford Inn and Poosie Nansie's hostelry saw him cross swords with the Kirk Session and he and his friend James Smith, a local draper, were formally censured for 'fornication', this being listed as a mortal sin in the eyes of the Church.

The trilogy was in a way Burns's response to this public shaming. Humour and courage were his chosen weapons against Satan and against a Church which served up a satanic God incapable of being the forgiving father Burns believed him to be. To Burns, the devil was only a myth to be exorcized with laughter. In this poem Satan is lectured about his foolish meddling in human affairs, his knuckles are rapped for interfering in Eden. By chiding, laughing at and finally showing sympathy towards the devil, Burns strips him of his elemental qualities and removes his menace. At the same time he strips the Church of its principal hold over a superstitious populace and consumes the nonsense of predestination in its own imaginary fires.

Address to the Deil

O Prince! O chief of many thronèd pow'rs!
That led th' embattl'd seraphim to war. – MILTON

O THOU! whatever title suit thee –
Auld 'Hornie,' 'Satan,' 'Nick,' or 'Clootie,'
Wha in yon cavern grim an' sootie,
Clos'd under hatches,
Spairges about the   dashes –
    brunstane cootie,   pail of brimstone
To scaud poor wretches!   scald

Hear me, auld 'Hangie,' for a wee,
An' let poor damnèd bodies be;
I'm sure sma' pleasure it can gie,
Ev'n to a deil,
To skelp an' scaud poor dogs   slap – unmanageable
    like me,
An' hear us squeel!

Great is thy pow'r an' great thy fame;
Far kenn'd an' noted is thy name;
An' tho' yon lowin heugh's thy hame,   burning pit
Thou travels far;
An' faith! thou's neither lag nor lame,   slow
Nor blate, nor scaur.   bashful – apt to be scared

Whyles, rangin like a roarin lion,
For prey, a' holes an' corners tryin;
Whyles, on the strong-wing'd tempest flyin,
Tirlin the kirks;   Unroofing – churches
Whyles, in the human bosom pryin,
Unseen thou lurks.

I've heard my rev'rend grannie say,
In lanely glens ye like to stray;
Or where auld ruin'd castles grey
Nod to the moon,
Ye fright the nightly wand'rer's way,
Wi' eldritch croon.   weird

When twilight did my grannie summon,
To say her pray'rs, douse, honest woman!
Aft 'yont the dyke she's heard you bummin,
Wi' eerie drone;
Or, rustlin', thro' the boortrees comin,   elder-trees
Wi' heavy groan.

Ae dreary, windy, winter night,
The stars shot down wi' sklentin light,   slanting
Wi' you mysel, I gat a fright,
Ayont the lough;
Ye, like a rash-buss, stood in sight,   tuft of rushes
Wi' wavin sough.   sound

The cudgel in my nieve did shake,   fist
Each bristl'd hair stood like a stake,
When wi' an eldritch, stoor 'quaick,   deep-voiced
   quaick',
Amang the springs,
Awa ye squatter'd like a
   drake,   noisy flight of a wild duck
On whistlin wings.

Let warlocks grim, an' wither'd hags,
Tell how wi' you, on ragweed nags,   ragwort
They skim the muirs an' dizzy crags,   moors
Wi' wicked speed;
And in kirk-yards renew their leagues,
Owre howket dead.   dug-up

Thence, countra wives, wi' toil an' pain,
May plunge an' plunge the kirn in vain;   churn
For oh! the yellow treasures taen
By witchin skill;
An' dawtet, twal-pint 'hawkie's' gane   petted – cow
As yell's the bill.   milkless as the bull

Thence, mystic knots mak great abuse
On young guidmen, fond, keen an'
   croose;   confident
When the best wark-lume i' the house,
By cantraip wit,   magic
Is instant made no worth a louse,
Just at the bit.

When thowes dissolve the snawy hoord,   thaws
An' float the jinglin icy boord,
Then, water-kelpies haunt the   water-spirits –
   foord,   ford
By your direction,
And 'nighted trav'llers are allur'd   benighted
To their destruction.

And aft your moss-traversin
   'Spunkies'   Will-o'-the-wisps
Decoy the wight that late an' drunk is:
The bleezin, curst, mischievous monkies
Delude his eyes,
Till in some miry slough he sunk is,
Ne'er mair to rise.

When masons' mystic word an' grip
In storms an' tempests raise you up,
Some cock or cat your rage maun stop,
Or, strange to tell!
The youngest 'brither' ye wad whip
Aff straught to hell.

Lang syne in Eden's bonie yard,   garden
When youthfu' lovers first were pair'd,
An' all the soul of love they shar'd,
The raptur'd hour –
Sweet on the fragrant flow'ry swaird,   sward
In shady bow'r;

Then you, ye auld, snick-drawin dog!
Ye cam to Paradise *incog,*
An' play'd on man a cursèd brogue,   trick
(Black be your fa'!)
An' gied the infant warld a shog,   shake
'Maist ruin'd a'.

D'ye mind that day when in a bizz   bustle
Wi' reeket duds, an' reestet
   gizz,   smoked clothes – withered appearance
Ye did present your smootie phiz   dirty face
'Mang better folk,
An' sklented on the man of Uzz   cast
Your spitefu' joke?

An' how ye gat him i' your thrall,
An' brak him out o' house an' hal',
While scabs an' blotches did him gall,
Wi' bitter claw;
An' lows'd his ill-tongu'd, wicked
   scaul –   scolding wife
Was warst ava?

But a' your doings to rehearse,
Your wily snares an' fechtin fierce,
Sin' that day Michael did you pierce,
Down to this time,
Wad ding a Lallan tongue,   be too much for –
   or Erse,   Lowland Scots – Irish Gaelic
In prose or rhyme.

An now, auld 'Cloots,' I ken ye're thinkin,
A certain bardie's rantin, drinkin,
Some luckless hour will send him linkin,
To your black pit;
But, faith! he'll turn a corner jinkin,   dodging
An' cheat you yet.

But fare-you-weel, auld 'Nickie-ben!'
O wad ye tak a thought an' men'!
Ye aiblins might – I dinna ken –   perhaps
Still hae a stake:
I'm wae to think upo' yon den,
Ev'n for your sake!

22

Address to the Unco Guid, or the Rigidly Righteous

Written in 1786, probably after Burns had been disciplined for fornication by the Kirk Session of Mauchline Parish Church, the poem is not so much a plea for human frailty as the poet cocking a snook at the self-righteous burghers of Mauchline. Debunking the sanctimonious was one of Burns's favourite themes and if we look back to 1784 and into his First Commonplace Book, where he jotted down his thoughts and ideas about life, we can see the seeds of this later work:

Let any of the strictest character for regularity of conduct among us, examine impartially how many of his virtues are owing to constitution and education; how many vices he has never been guilty of, not from any care or vigilance, but from want of opportunity, or some accidental circumstance intervening; how many of the weaknesses of mankind he has escaped because he was out of line of such temptation; and, what often, if not always, weighs more than all the rest; how much he is indebted to the world's good opinion because the world does not know all: I say any man who can thus think, will scan the failings nay the faults and crimes, of mankind around him, with a brother's eye.

Address to the Unco Guid, or the Rigidly Righteous

My son, these Maxims make a rule,
And lump them ay thegither;   together
The *Rigid Righteous* is a fool,
The *Rigid Wise* anither:
The cleanest corn that e'er was
  dight   thrashed or winnowed
May hae some pyles o' caff in   grains – chaff
So ne'er a fellow-creature slight
For random fits o' daffin.   merriment, folly
                          SOLOMON – Eccles. vii. 16.

O ye wha are sae guid yoursel,
Sae pious and sae holy,
Ye've nought to do but mark and tell
Your Neebour's fauts and folly!   faults
Whase life is like a weel-gaun mill,   well-going
Supply'd wi' store o' water,
The heapèt happer's ebbing still,   hopper
And still the clap plays clatter.

Hear me, ye venerable Core,   folk
As counsel for poor mortals,
That frequent pass douce Wisdom's door   grave
For glaikit Folly's portals;   careless
I, for their thoughtless, careless sakes,
Would here propone defences,
Their donsie tricks, their black mistakes,   unlucky
Their failings and mischances.

Ye see your state wi' theirs compar'd,
And shudder at the niffer,   comparison
But cast a moment's fair regard,
What maks the mighty differ;   difference
Discount what scant occasion gave,
That purity ye pride in,
And (what's aft mair than a' the   often more –
  lave)   rest
Your better art o' hiding.

24

Think, when your castigated pulse
Gies now and then a wallop,   *plunge, flourish*
What ragings must his veins convulse,
That still eternal gallop:
Wi' wind and tide fair i' your tail,
Right on ye scud your sea-way;
But in the teeth o' baith to sail,   *both*
It maks an unco leeway.   *terrible*

See Social-life and Glee sit down,
All joyous and unthinking,
Till, quite transmugrify'd, they're   *transformed*
  grown
Debauchery and Drinking:
O would they stay to calculate
Th' eternal consequences;
Or your more dreaded h—ll to state,
D—mnation of expences!

Ye high, exalted, virtuous Dames,
Ty'd up in godly laces,
Before ye gie poor *Frailty* names,
Suppose a change o' cases;
A dear-lov'd lad, convenience snug,
A treacherous inclination –
But, let me whisper i' your lug,   *ear*
Ye're aiblins nae temptation.   *perhaps*

Then gently scan your brother Man,
Still gentler sister Woman;
Tho' they may gang a kennin wrang,
To step aside is human:
One point must still be greatly dark,
The moving *Why* they do it;
And just as lamely can ye mark,
How far perhaps they rue it.

Who made the heart, 'tis *He* alone
Decidedly can try us,
He knows each chord its various tone.
Each spring its various bias:
Then at the balance let's be mute,
We never can adjust it;
What's *done* we partly may compute
But know not what's *resisted*.

25

Ae Fond Kiss

Agnes McLehose first met Burns in December 1787 during his second winter in Edinburgh. After experiencing the traditional reserve of the Edinburgh ladies, Burns was charmed by this enthusiastic amateur poetess (it was on her suggestion that the Arcadian names Clarinda and Sylvander were used in their future correspondence). A vivacious, attractive woman of twenty-nine, Agnes was living alone with her three children in Potterrow, her errant drunken husband, the lawyer James McLehose, having been dispatched to Jamaica by her well-connected relatives. Their next meeting was postponed for three weeks after Burns suffered a knee injury in a coach accident and this is when their famous, passionate correspondence began.

On his first visit to Potterrow Burns was soon made to understand that because of Clarinda's staunch Calvinist beliefs their fervent declarations of love must remain on a purely platonic basis. Nevertheless the 'affair' continued. But not without stirring up gossip. Burns's visits to her home were noted and Agnes was advised by friends to abandon the alliance. An incensed Burns at first came to her support with even more heated assurances of undying devotion, but less than two months later it was he who ended the relationship. Jean Armour had given birth to their second set of twins and by April of 1788 Burns and she were married by mutual declaration, a traditional and binding form of contract in Scotland at that time. How Clarinda found out we do not know. But she wrote Burns a less than loving missive accusing him of villainy in his conduct towards her.

In November 1791 Clarinda and Sylvander met again in Edinburgh for the last time, shortly before she sailed to Jamaica to attempt a reconciliation with her husband. On returning to Dumfries he wrote 'Ae Fond Kiss' and, dropping the Arcadian names, sent it to 'my dearest Nancy' the old wounds healed and the passion replaced with friendship. Agnes McLehose left for Jamaica in

February 1792, but returned in August on the same ship, having found her husband unchanged in his habits and now the father of several more children. She died in 1841 at the age of eighty-two. In her declining years she altered the more ardent passages in Burns's letters and eventually had to sell some for a few shillings to support herself.

It was the opinion of Sir Walter Scott that the fourth verse of 'Ae Fond Kiss' was 'the essence of a thousand love tales'.

Ae Fond Kiss

TUNE – *Rory Dall's Port*

Ae fond kiss, and then we sever;   One
Ae fareweel, and then for ever!
Deep in heart-wrung tears I'll pledge thee,
Warring sighs and groans I'll wage thee.

Who shall say that Fortune grieves him
While the star of hope she leaves him?
Me, nae cheerful twinkle lights me:
Dark despair around benights me.

I'll ne'er blame my partial fancy,
Naething could resist my Nancy:
But to see her was to love her;
Love but her, and love for ever.

Had we never lov'd sae kindly!
Had we never lov'd sae blindly!
Never met – or never parted,
We had ne'er been broken-hearted.

Fare-thee-weel, thou first and fairest!
Fare-thee-weel, thou best and dearest!
Thine be ilka joy and treasure,   every
Peace, Enjoyment, Love and Pleasure!

Ae fond kiss, and then we sever!
Ae fareweel, Alas, for ever!
Deep in heart-wrung tears I'll pledge thee,
Warring sighs and groans I'll wage thee.

Afton Water

Mary Campbell, the inspiration for this song, first met the poet early in 1786. A young dairy maid at Montgomerie Castle (Coilsfield House), she was a regular attender at Tarbolton Church, where she first caught Burns's eye. Better known as 'Highland Mary' for her Gaelic pronunciation of the Bible, she became involved with Burns at a turbulent time in his life. He was preparing the Kilmarnock edition of his poems for publication, considering emigration to Jamaica and Jean Armour was pregnant by him. Jean's father had refused his marriage offer, preferring instead to issue a writ to secure a financial settlement for his daughter and her child rather than to see her marry an unsuccessful farmer, unknown rhymster and well-known rake. Burns's letters well document his anger and frustration with Jean and her family.

This raises the question of whether Burns turned to Mary because of his rejection by the Armour family or was he in fact pursuing both women at the same time? Whatever the circumstances, he did appear to be deeply in love with Mary in May of that year. On the second Sunday of the month, before she returned to Campbeltown to visit relatives, they performed an ancient Scottish custom of plighting their troth by exchanging Bibles across a stream. It was to be their last meeting. Mary died in October in Greenock of a fever. There has been a great deal of conjecture as to whether Burns intended to take Mary to Jamaica as his wife and if her death was due to childbirth and not to typhus as was recorded. Certainly Burns's feelings of guilt about her lasted for many years. He was reticent in speaking about her and letters which might have shed light on their relationship were burned by her brother to prevent any embarrassment to her family.

Apart from 'Afton Water' (written in 1789), Burns dedicated other works to Mary including 'To Mary in Heaven' and 'Highland Mary'.

Afton Water

I charge you, O ye daughters of Jerusalem, that ye stir not, nor awake my love – my dove, my undefiled! The flowers appear on the earth, the time of the singing of the birds is come, and the voice of the turtle is heard in our land. – *R. B.*

Tune – *The Yellow-haired Laddie*

Flow gently, sweet Afton, among thy green
    braes,   hill-slope
Flow gently, I'll sing thee a song in thy praise;
My Mary's asleep by the murmuring stream,
Flow gently, sweet Afton, disturb not her dream.

Thou stock dove whose echo resounds thro' the
    glen,
Ye wild whistling blackbirds in yon thorny den,
Thou green crested lapwing thy screaming
    forbear,
I charge you disturb not my slumbering Fair.

How lofty, sweet Afton, thy neighbouring hills,
Far mark'd with the courses of clear, winding rills;
There daily I wander as noon rises high,
My flocks and my Mary's sweet Cot in my eye.

How pleasant thy banks and green vallies below,
Where, wild in the woodlands, the primroses
    blow;
There oft as mild ev'ning weeps over the lea,
The sweet-scented birk shades my Mary   birch
    and me.

The crystal stream, Afton, how lovely it glides,
And winds by the cot where my Mary resides;
How wanton thy waters her snowy feet lave,
As, gathering sweet flowerets, she stems thy
    clear wave.

Flow gently, sweet Afton, among thy green
    braes,
Flow gently, sweet River, the theme of my lays;
My Mary's asleep by thy murmuring stream,
Flow gently, sweet Afton, disturb not her dream.

A Red, Red Rose

Burns altered and improved the original version of this song which he wrote in 1794. It was believed to have been written by a Lieutenant Hinches as a farewell to his sweetheart. By combining it with another 'farewell' discovered in an old anthology, he created a song of such enduring sentiment that although it was denigrated by his critics, it still remains one of his best-loved works.

A Red, Red Rose

Tune – *Graham's Strathspey*

O my Luve's like a red, red rose
That's newly sprung in June;
O my Luve's like the melodie
That's sweetly play'd in tune.
As fair art thou, my bonie lass,
So deep in luve am I;
And I will luve thee still, my dear,
Till a' the seas gang dry.

Till a' the seas gang dry, my Dear,
And the rocks melt wi' the sun;
O I will love thee still, my dear,
While the sands o' life shall run.
And fare thee weel, my only Luve!
And fare thee weel a while!
And I will come again, my Luve,
Tho' it were ten thousand mile!

Auld Lang Syne

Burns added the third and fourth verses to this ancient air making it universally his own. He composed his version of the song in 1788. Now an international anthem, it is sung at the close of gatherings all over the world. Its charm lies in the easy intimacy and simplicity of the lyrics, the remembrance of old friendships and the desire to be transported back to the days of childhood.

Auld Lang Syne

Should auld acquaintance be forgot,   old
And never brought to mind?
Should auld acquaintance be forgot,
And auld lang syne!   days of long ago

Chorus – For auld lang syne, my dear,
    For auld lang syne,
    We'll tak a cup o' kindness yet
    For auld lang syne.

And surely ye'll be your pint stowp!   tankard
And surely I'll be mine!
And we'll tak a cup o' kindness yet,
For auld lang syne.

We twa hae run about the braes,
And pou'd the gowans fine: pulled
But we've wander'd mony a weary fitt, many – foot
Sin' auld lang syne.   Since

We twa hae paidl'd in the burn   waded
Frae morning sun till dine: dinner-time
But seas between us braid hae roar'd broad
Sin' auld lang syne.

And there's a hand, my trusty fiere!   friend
And gie's a hand o' thine!   give
And we'll tak a right gude-willie waught draught
For auld lang syne.

Bruce to his Men at Bannockburn

In 1314 King Edward II's 18000-strong army was resoundingly defeated by Robert the Bruce's 8000 men at the Battle of Bannockburn. Burns composed this imaginery address by Bruce to his soldiers on the morning of the battle, setting it to the air 'Hey, tuttie taitie', believed to be Bruce's marching tune. Burns said it often moved him to tears. He visited the site of the battle in 1787 and visualized his 'gallant, heroic countrymen, coming o'er the hill and down upon the plunderers of their country.'

Burns composed the song in September 1793 and sent it to George Thomson for his *Select Scottish Airs.* Thomson persuaded him to change the tune to 'Lewie Gordon', but public demand ensured that Burns's original choice was reinstated.

Bruce to his Men at Bannockburn

TUNE – *Hey, tuttie taitie*

Scots, wha hae wi' Wallace bled,   who have
Scots, wham Bruce has aften led,   whom
Welcome to your gory bed
Or to victorie!

Now's the day, and now's the hour;
See the front of battle lour;
See approach proud Edward's power –
Chains and slaverie!

Wha will be a traitor-knave?
Wha can fill a coward's grave?
Wha sae base as be a slave?
Let him turn and flee!

Wha for Scotland's king and law
Freedom's sword will strongly draw,
Freeman stand, or freeman fa',
Let him follow me!

By oppression's woes and pains!
By your sons in servile chains!
We will drain our dearest veins,
But they shall be free!

Lay the proud usurpers low!
Tyrants fall in ev'ry foe!
Liberty's in ev'ry blow! –
Let us do or die!

Coming through the Rye

A well-known and popular song to this day, this image of a young woman sauntering through fields of rye on a summer's afternoon seems essentially Burns. Reworked from an old song, it was written during August 1794 and first published in 1796 after the poet's death. The later version has Jenny as the singer of the song:

> Ilka lassie has her laddie,
> Nane they say ha'e I;
> Yet a' the lads they smile at me
> When comin' thro' the rye.
>
> *Chorus*

Coming through the Rye

TUNE – *Coming through the Rye*

Coming through the rye, poor body,
Coming through the rye,
She draiglet a' her petticoatie,   wet
Coming through the rye.

Chorus – Jenny's a' wat, poor body,
              Jenny's seldom dry;
              She draiglet a' her petticoatie,
              Coming through the rye.

Gin a body meet a body   If
Coming through the rye,
Gin a body kiss a body,
Need a body cry?

Gin a body meet a body
Coming through the glen,
Gin a body kiss a body,
Need the world ken?

Death and Dr Hornbook

Having endured a boring evening at the Free-masons' Lodge in Tarbolton listening to the endless prattle of John Wilson, an amateur medical man, on the efficacy of his cures, Burns was driven to write this supernatural, satirical jibe. In the poem the drunken narrator meets Death on the road one moonlit night and has to listen to his complaints about losing most of his business to a Doctor Hornbook, whose medicines are so effective in killing people off that Death has been made redundant. The doctor is more deadly than Death himself and Death is feeling cheated.

Wilson was by profession not a doctor, but a parish schoolteacher in Tarbolton, though he also sold groceries and drugs to supplement his tiny income. Despite the fact that he became a laughing-stock after the poem was published in 1786, Wilson bore no ill-feeling towards Burns; in fact he later attributed his comfortable lifestyle to the notoriety the poem had brought him. Leaving Tarbolton after a dispute about his salary, he settled in Glasgow, where he taught successfully and in 1807 became Session Clerk for the Gorbals, at that time a suburb of Glasgow.

Death and Dr Hornbook

A True Story

Some books are lies frae end to end,
And some great lies were never penn'd:
Ev'n ministers they hae been kenn'd,
In holy rapture,
A rousing whid at times to vend,   *fib*
And nail't wi' Scripture.

But this that I am gaun to tell,   *going*
Which lately on a night befel,
Is just as true's the Deil's in hell
Or Dublin city:
That e'er he nearer comes oursel
'S a muckle pity.

The clachan yill had made me   *village ale*
   canty,   *merry*
I was na fou, but just had plenty;   *drunk*
I stacher'd whyles, but yet took   *staggered at times*
   tent ay   *care*
To free the ditches;
An' hillocks, stanes, an' bushes, kenn'd ay
Frae ghaists an' witches.

The rising moon began to glowre   *stare*
The distant *Cumnock* hills out-owre:
To count her horns, wi' a' my pow'r,
I set mysel;
But whether she had three or four,
I cou'd na tell.

I was come round about the hill,
An' todlin down on *Willie's mill*,   *tottering*
Setting my staff wi' a' my skill,
To keep me sicker;   *secure*
Tho' leeward whyles, against my will,   *sometimes*
I took a bicker.   *short race*

I there wi' *Something* did forgather,
That pat me in an eerie swither;   frightened hesitation
An awfu' scythe, out-owre ae shouther,
Clear-dangling, hang;
A three-tae'd leister on the ither   fish-spear
Lay, large an' lang.

Its stature seem'd lang Scotch ells twa,
The queerest shape that e'er I saw,
For fient a wame it had ava;   Deuce! – belly
And then its shanks,
They were as thin, as sharp an' sma'
As cheeks o' branks.

'Guid e'en,' quo' I; 'Friend, hae ye
    been mawin,   mowing
'When ither folk are busy sawin?'   sowing
It seem'd to make a kind o' stan',
But naething spak;
At length, says I: 'Friend! whare ye gaun?
'Will ye go back?'

It spak right howe, – 'My name is *Death*,   hollow
'But be na' fley'd.' – Quoth I, 'Guid   frightened
    faith,
'Ye're may be come to stap my breath;
'But tent me, billie;   give heed to me – comrade
'I red ye weel, tak care o' skaith,   advise – harm
'See, there's a gully!'   clasp-knife

'Gudeman,' quo' he, 'put up your whittle,   knife
'I'm no design'd to try its mettle;
'But if I did, I wad be kittle   apt
'To be mislear'd;   rude
'I wad na mind it, no that spittle
'Out-owre my beard.'

'Weel, weel!' says I, 'a bargain be't;
'Come, gies your hand, an' sae we're
    gree't;   agreed
'We'll ease our shanks an' tak a seat –   limbs
'Come, gie's your news;
'This while ye hae been mony a gate,   road
'At mony a house.'

39

'Ay, ay!' quo' he, an' shook his head,
'It's e'en a lang, lang time indeed
'Sin' I began to nick the thread,   cut
'An' choke the breath:
'Folk maun do something for their bread,
'An' sae maun *Death*.

'Sax thousand years are near-hand fled
'Sin' I was to the butching bred,   butcher's trade
'An' mony a scheme in vain's been laid,
'To stap or scar me;   stop – scare
'Till ane *Hornbook's* ta'en up the trade,
'And faith! he'll waur me.   worst

'Ye ken *Jock Hornbook* i' the Clachan –   village
'Deil mak his king's-hood in a
    spleuchan! –   tobacco-pouch
'He's grown sae weel acquaint wi' *Buchan*
'And ither chaps,
'The weans haud out their fingers laughin, children
'An pouk my hips.   pluck

'See, here's a scythe, an' there's a dart,
'They hae pierc'd mony a gallant heart;
'But Doctor *Hornbook* wi' his art
'An cursèd skill,
'Has made them baith no worth a f—t,
'D—n'd haet they'll kill!   they will not kill anything

''Twas but yestreen, nae farther gane,   yesterday
'I threw a noble throw at ane;
'Wi' less, I'm sure, I've hundreds slain;
'But deil-ma-care,   no matter
'It just play'd dirl on the
    bane,   a short tremulous stroke
'But did nae mair.

'*Hornbook* was by, wi' ready art,
'An' had sae fortify'd the part,
'That when I lookèd to my dart,
'It was sae blunt,
'Fient haet o' 't wad hae pierc'd the heart   not a bit
'Of a kail-runt.   stalk of green kale

'I drew my scythe in sic a fury,
'I near-hand cowpit wi' my hurry,   tumbled over
'But yet the bauld *Apothecary*
'Withstoood the shock;
'I might as well hae try'd a quarry
'O' hard whin rock.

'Ev'n them he canna get attended,
'Altho' their face he ne'er had kend it,
'Just —— in a kail-blade, an' send it,
'As soon 's he smells 't,
'Baith their disease, and what will mend it,
'At once he tells 't.

'And then a' doctor's saws an' whittles   knives
'Of a' dimensions, shapes, an' mettles,
'A' kind o' boxes, mugs, an' bottles,
'He's sure to hae;
'Their Latin names as fast he rattles
'As A B C.

'Calces o' fossils, earths, and trees;
'True sal-marinum o' the seas;
'The farina of beans an' pease,
'He has 't in plenty;
'Aqua-fontis, what you please,
'He can content ye.

'Forbye some new, uncommon weapons,
'Urinus spiritus of capons;
'Or mite-horn shavings, filings, scrapings,
'Distill'd *per se*;
'Sal-alkali o' midge-tail-clippings,
'And mony mae.'

'Wae's me for *Johnie Ged's Hole* now,'
Quoth I, 'if that thae news be true!
'His braw calf-ward where gowans grew   daisies
'Sae white and bonie,
'Nae doubt they'll rive it wi' the   tear it up
   plew,   plough
'They'll ruin *Johnie!*'

The creature grain'd an eldritch laugh,   *unearthly*
And says, 'Ye needna yoke the pleugh,
'Kirkyards will soon be till'd eneugh,
'Take ye na fear:
'They'll a' be trenched wi' mony a sheugh,   *furrow*
'In twa-three year.

'Whare I kill'd ane, a fair strae
    death,   *death in (a straw) bed*
'By loss o' blood or want of breath,
'This night I'm free to take my aith,
'That *Hornbook's* skill
'Has clad a score i' their last claith,   *grave-cloth*
'By drap an' pill.   *potion*

'An honest wabster to his trade,   *weaver*
'Whase wife's twa nieves were scarce   *fists*
    weel-bred,
'Gat tippence-worth to mend her head,
'When it was sair;
'The wife slade cannie to her bed,   *slid gently*
'But ne'er spak mair.

'A country laird had ta'en the batts,   *colic*
'Or some curmurring in his
    guts,   *slight attack of the gripes*
'His only son for *Hornbook* sets,
'An' pays him well:
'The lad, for twa guid gimmer-pets,   *young ewes*
'Was laird himsel.

'A bonie lass – ye kend her name –
'Some ill-brewn drink had hov'd her wame:
'She trusts hersel, to hide the shame,
'In *Hornbook's* care;
'*Horn* sent her aff to her lang hame,
'To hide it there.

'That's just a swatch o' *Hornbook's* way;   *example*
'Thus goes he on from day to day,
'Thus does he poison, kill, an' slay,
'An's weel paid for't;
'Yet stops me o' my lawfu' prey,
'Wi' his d—d dirt:

'But, hark! I'll tell you of a plot,
'Tho' dinna ye be speaking o' 't;
'I'll nail the self-conceited sot,
'As dead's a herrin:
'Niest time we meet, I'll wad a groat,   wager
'He gets his fairin!'   reward

But just as he began to tell,
The auld kirk-hammer strak the bell   struck
Some wee short hour ayont the *twal*,   twelve
Which rais'd us baith: roused
I took the way that pleas'd mysel,
And sae did *Death*.

43

A Man's a Man for a' that

By the time Burns wrote this composition in 1795 the panic felt by the British government over the French Revolution had largely subsided. Always a blunt, outspoken man, Burns had voiced his approval of the American and French Revolutions to such an extent that he was in danger of losing his excise post. He was subsequently advised by friends to tone down his republican sympathies. Perhaps he did mellow, but only slightly and towards the end of his life his energy and passion for Liberty and Equality remained undiminished. His beliefs, although now tinged with sadness, have an even greater sureness.

A Man's a Man for a' that

Is there for honest Poverty
That hings his head, and a' that?   all that
The coward-slave, we pass him by,
We dare be poor for a' that!
For a' that, and a' that,
Our toils obscure, and a' that,
The rank is but the guinea's stamp,
The Man's the gowd for a' that!

What though on hamely fare we dine,
Wear hoddin grey, and a' that;   coarse cloth
Gie fools their silks and knaves their wine,
A Man's a Man for a' that:
For a' that, and a' that,
Their tinsel show, and a' that;
The honest man, tho' e'er sae poor,
Is king o' men for a' that!

Ye see yon birkie ca'd a lord   fellow
Wha struts, and stares, and a' that,
Though hundreds worship at his word,
He's but a coof for a' that: fool, ninny
For a' that, and a' that,
His ribband, star and a' that;
The man of independent mind
He looks and laughs at a' that.

A prince can mak a belted knight,
A marquis, duke and a' that;
But an honest man's aboon his might —   above
Gude faith, he mauna fa' that!   must not
For a' that, and a' that,
Their dignities, and a' that;
The pith o' sense and pride o' worth
Are higher rank than a' that.

Then let us pray that come it may, —
As come it will for a' that —
That Sense and Worth, o'er a' the earth,
May bear the gree, and a' that.   supremacy
For a' that, and a' that,
It's comin' yet for a' that,
That Man to Man, the world o'er,
Shall brothers be for a' that!

Holy Willie's Prayer

Burns's glorious hypocrite 'Holy Willie' is still instantly recognizable today. With wonderful irony, he delivers a lash upon his own back in every line. One of Burns's finest pieces of work, it was written in the summer of 1785 when his landlord and friend Gavin Hamilton was finally absolved by higher Church courts of not keeping the Sabbath. The chief instigator of the prosecution was William Fisher, a Church elder and member of the Kirk Session of Mauchline Parish Church, which first 'tried' Hamilton for such crimes as picking potatoes on Sunday and not attending Church. A Mauchline man by birth, Hamilton lived there with his wife and young family, practising as a lawyer and administering the poor fund. A kind-hearted and generous friend to many, he was the very antitheses of William Fisher.

Fisher, born the son of a farmer in 1737, became an elder of Mauchline Church in 1772. A gossiping, smug, zealous upholder of strict Calvinist tenets, he came unstuck in 1790, when he was

publicly rebuked by the minister William Auld for drunkenness, and although there is no church record, it is also believed that he was charged with stealing from the poor box. He froze to death in a ditch near Mauchline on 13 February 1809.

Burns initially circulated the poem amongst friends as it was considered too strident an attack on the Church to be published. It was only in 1799, three years after his death, that it was finally printed and then only as a leaflet by a Glasgow publisher.

Holy Willie's Prayer

And Send the Godly in a pet to pray. – POPE

O Thou that in the heavens does dwell!
Wha, as it pleases best Thysel,
Sends ane to heaven and ten to h–ll,
A' for Thy glory;
And no for ony guid or ill
They've done before Thee!

I bless and praise Thy matchless might
When thousands Thou hast left in night,
That I am here before Thy sight,
For gifts and grace
A burning and a shining light,
To a' this place.

What was I, or my generation,
That I should get such exaltation?
I, wha deserv'd most just damnation
For broken laws,
Sax thousand years ere my creation
Thro' Adam's cause.

When frae my mither's womb I fell,
Thou might hae plungèd me in hell,
To gnash my gums, to weep and wail,
In burnin lakes,
Where damnèd devils roar and yell,
Chain'd to their stakes.

Yet I am here, a chosen sample,
To show Thy grace is great and ample
I'm here, a pillar o' Thy temple,
Strong as a rock;
A guide, a ruler, and example
To a' Thy flock.

O L–d, Thou kens what zeal I bear,
When drinkers drink, an' swearers swear,
An' singin' there, an' dancin' here,
Wi' great and sma';
For I am keepit by Thy fear,
Free frae them a'.

But yet, O L–d, confess I must,
At times I'm fash'd wi' fleshly lust;   troubled
And sometimes too in warldly trust
Vile Self gets in:
But Thou remembers we are dust,
Defil'd wi' sin.

O L–d – yestreen – Thou kens – wi Meg –
Thy pardon I sincerely beg:
O, may't ne'er be a livin plague,
To my dishonor!
And I'll ne'er lift a lawless leg
Again upon her!

Besides, I further maun avow,
Wi' Leezie's lass – three times – I trow –
But L–d, that Friday I was fou   drunk
When I cam near her;
Or else, Thou kens, Thy servant true
Wad never steer her.   meddle with

Maybe Thou lets this fleshly thorn
Buffet Thy servant e'en and morn
Lest he owre proud and high should turn
That he's sae gifted:
If sae, Thy hand maun e'en be borne
Until Thou lift it.

L–d bless Thy chosen in this place,
For here Thou has a chosen race;
But G–d confound their stubborn face,
And blast their name,
Wha bring their rulers to disgrace
And public shame.

L–d mind Gaun Hamilton's deserts;
He drinks, and swears, and plays at cartes,   cards
Yet has sae mony takin arts   popular
Wi' Great and Sma',
Frae G–d's ain Priest the people's hearts
He steals awa.

And when we chasten'd him therefore
Thou kens how he bred sic a splore,   disturbance
And set the warld in a roar
O' laughin at us:
Curse Thou his basket and his store
Kail and potatoes.

L–d hear my earnest cry and pray'r
Against that Presbytry of Ayr!
Thy strong right hand, L–d make it bare
Upo' their heads!
L–d visit them and dinna spare,
For their misdeeds!

O L–d, my G–d, that glib-tongu'd Aiken,
My very heart and flesh are quakin,
To think how I sat, sweatin, shakin,
And —— wi' dread,
While Auld, wi' hingin lip gaed sneakin   sneaky
And hid his head.

L–d in Thy day o' vengeance try him!
L–d visit them wha did employ him!
And pass not in Thy mercy by them,
Nor hear their prayer,
But for Thy people's sake destroy them,
And dinna spare!

But L–d remember me and mine
Wi' mercies temporal and divine;
That I for grace and gear may shine,
Excell'd by nane!
And a' the glory shall be Thine,
AMEN! AMEN!

John Anderson, my Jo

The original version of this song has been found in a sixteenth-century manuscript. Burns changed it in 1790 from a rather bawdy verse into a tender depiction of love through the passage of time.

John Anderson, my Jo

TUNE – *John Anderson, my Jo*

John Anderson, my jo, John	love, darling
When we were first acquent,	
Your locks were like the raven,	
Your bonie brow was brent;	unwrinkled
But now your brow is beld, John,	bald
Your locks are like the snaw;	
But blessings on your frosty pow,	white head
John Anderson, my jo.	

John Anderson, my jo, John,	
We clamb the hill thegither;	climbed
And mony a canty day, John,	happy
We've had wi' ane anither;	
Now we maun totter down, John:	
And hand in hand we'll go,	
And sleep thegither at the foot,	
John Anderson, my Jo.	

Lines written on the Window of a Room in Stirling

At the beginning of his second tour of the Highlands in August 1787, Burns visited Stirling Castle, previously the scene of many Scottish parliaments. Irate at the poor condition of the ancient hall, he scratched this message on a window of the inn where he was staying, as an insulting gesture to the Hanoverian monarchy. It was to cause him a great deal of trouble, so much so that two months later he returned and knocked out the glass, but the damage was done, it had already been copied and circulated.

Lines written on the Window of a Room in Stirling

Here Stewarts once in glory reigned,
And laws for Scotland's weal ordained;
But now unroofed their palace stands,
Their sceptre's swayed by other hands;
Fallen, indeed, and to the earth
Whence grovelling reptiles take their birth,
The injured Stewart line is gone,
A race outlandish fills their throne;
An idiot race, to honour lost;
Who know them best despise them most.

Rash mortal, and slanderous Poet, thy name
Shall no longer appear in the records of fame;
Dost not know that old Mansfield, who writes like
the Bible,
Says the more 'tis a truth, Sir, the more 'tis a libel?

Angry at William Nicol's criticism of his lack of wisdom in writing the first verse, Burns added the last four lines by way of a tongue-in-cheek reprimand to himself.

John Barleycorn

Founded on an ancient ballad, Burns in 1785 produced this amusing, allegorical tribute to the bold qualities bestowed by whisky. It is a celebration of the harvest, of whisky and of life itself.

John Barleycorn

A BALLAD

There was three kings into the east,
Three kings both great and high,
And they hae sworn a solemn oath
John Barleycorn should die.

They took a plough and plough'd him down,
Put clods upon his head,
And they hae sworn a solemn oath
John Barleycorn was dead.

But the cheerful Spring came kindly on,
And show'rs began to fall;
John Barleycorn got up again,
And sore surpris'd them all.

The sultry suns of Summer came,
And he grew thick and strong;
His head weel arm'd wi' pointed spears
That no one should him wrong.

The sober Autumn enter'd mild,
When he grew wan and pale;
His bending joints and drooping head
Show'd he began to fail.

His colour sicken'd more and more,
He faded into age;
And then his enemies began
To show their deadly rage.

They've taen a weapon, long and sharp,
And cut him by the knee;
Then ty'd him fast upon a cart,
Like a rogue for forgerie.

They laid him down upon his back,
And cudgell'd him full sore;
They hung him up before the storm,
And turn'd him o'er and o'er.

They fillèd up a darksome pit
With water to the brim,
They heavèd in John Barleycorn –
There let him sink or swim.

They laid him out upon the floor,
To work him further woe;
And still, as signs of life appear'd,
They toss'd him to and fro.

They wasted, o'er a scorching flame,
The marrow of his bones;
But a miller us'd him worst of all,
For he crush'd him 'tween two stones.

And they hae taen his very heart's blood,
And drank it round and round;
And still the more and more they drank,
Their joy did more abound.

John Barleycorn was a hero bold,
Of noble enterprise;
For if you do but taste his blood,
'Twill make your courage rise.

'Twill make a man forget his woe;
'Twill heighten all his joy:
'Twill make the widow's heart to sing,
Tho' the tear were in her eye.

Then let us toast John Barleycorn,
Each man a glass in hand;
And may his great posterity
Ne'er fail in old Scotland!

My Bonie Mary

Burns sent this ballad to his friend Mrs Dunlop on 17 December 1788 along with a copy of 'Auld Lang Syne', saying they were both old songs he had discovered. He later admitted that only the beginnings of both were old and the completed versions were his.

My Bonie Mary

Go, fetch to me a pint o' wine,
And fill it in a silver tassie,   cup
That I may drink, before I go,
A service to my bonie lassie:
The boat rocks at the Pier o' Leith,
Fu' loud the wind blaws frae the Ferry,   blows from
The ship rides by the Berwick-Law,
And I maun leave my bonie Mary.   must

The trumpets sound, the banners fly,
The glittering spears are rankèd ready,
The shouts o' war are heard afar,
The battle closes deep and bloody:
It's not the roar o' sea or shore
Wad make me langer wish to tarry;   Would – longer
Nor shouts o' war that's heard afar,
It's leaving thee, my bonie Mary!

O whistle, and I'll come to you, my Lad

Completed in 1793 during the Dumfriesshire years, this song was written for Jean Lorimer, a local beauty, daughter of a successful farmer, whose land lay across the River Nith from Ellisland. Burns later changed the last line of the chorus to 'Thy Jeanie will venture wi' you, my lad', saying Jean had insisted on it. A regular visitor to her home Kemmishall, Burns, undoubtedly inspired by her looks and spirited personality, described her as 'a fair dame whom the Graces have attired in witchcraft, and whom the Loves have armed with lightning'. She is 'The Lassie wi' the Lint-white Locks', the heroine of 'Craigieburn Wood' and his 'Chloris' in other songs. Sadly the fates which Burns saw as bestowing so many gifts upon her in youth, deserted her in later life.

At the age of eighteen, the year this song was finished, she refused an offer of marriage from one of Burns's fellow excise officers, choosing

instead to run away with a young Englishman named Whelpdale. After a wedding at Gretna Green they settled on a farm at Barnhill, near Moffat, but within a few months he went bankrupt and disappeared. She returned to her parents' home and seeming security, but her father lost his fortune and began drinking, leaving her finally reduced to working in service to support herself, dying in 1831 at the age of fifty-six.

O whistle, and I'll come to you, my Lad

TUNE – *O Whistle, and I'll come to you, my Lad*

Chorus – O whistle, and I'll come to you, my lad,
O whistle, and I'll come to you, my lad;
Tho' father and mother and a' should
gae mad,   go
O whistle, and I'll come to you, my lad.

But warily tent, when ye come to court me,   watch
And come na unless the back-yett be   gate –
a-jee;   ajar
Syne up the back-style, and let naebody see, Then
And come as ye were na coming to me,
And come as ye were na coming to me.

At kirk or at market, whene'er ye meet me,
Gang by me as tho' that ye car'd nae a flie; Go – fly
But steal me a blink o' your bonie black e'e, glance
Yet look as ye were na looking at me,
Yet look as ye were na looking at me.

Ay vow and protest that ye carena for me,
And *whyles* ye may lightly my   sometimes – under –
beauty a wee;   value – a little
But court na anither, tho' joking ye be,
For fear that she wyle your fancy frae me,   lure
For fear that she wyle your fancy frae me.

Poor Mailie's Elegy

This is one of two poems Burns wrote as a tribute to his pet ewe. Based on an incident at Lochlie farm when the animal was trapped in a ditch and almost strangled by her lead, they are both humorous and sentimental. The first composition 'The Death and Dying Words of Poor Mailie, the Author's Only Pet Yowe' was written immediately after the event; this he wrote some years later, from 1774 to 1784, just as he was putting the Kilmarnock edition of his work together.

Poor Mailie's Elegy

Lament in rhyme, lament in prose,
Wi' saut tears tricklin down your nose;
Our bardie's fate is at a close,
Past a' remead;   *remedy*
The last sad cape-stane o' his woe's
Poor Mailie's dead!

It's no the loss o' warl's gear,
That could sae bitter draw the tear,
Or make our bardie, dowie,
    wear   *borne down by grief*
The mournin weed:
He's lost a friend an' neebor dear.
In Mailie dead.

Thro' a' the town she trotted by him;
A lang half-mile she could descry him;
Wi' kindly bleat, when she did spy him,
She ran wi' speed:
A friend mair faithfu' ne'er cam nigh him,
Than Mailie dead.

I wat she was a sheep o' sense,
An' could behave hersel wi' mense: good manners
I'll say' t, she never brak a fence,
Thro' thievish greed.
Our bardie, lanely, keeps the spence   inner room
Sin' Mailie's dead.

Or, if he wanders up the howe,   valley
Her livin image in her yowe
Comes bleatin till him, owre the knowe,   knoll
For bits o' bread;
An' down the briny pearls rowe   roll
For Mailie dead.

She was nae get o' moorlan tips,   offspring – rams
Wi' tauted ket, an' hairy hips;   matted fleece
For her forbears were brought in ships   ancestors
Frae yont the Tweed:
A bonier fleesh ne'er cross'd the clips   fleece
Than Mailie's – dead.

Wae worth that man what first did shape
That vile, wanchancie thing – a raep!   ill-omened
It maks guid fellows girn an' gape,   make faces
Wi' chokin dread;
An' Robin's bonnet wave wi' crape
For Mailie dead.

O, a' ye bards on bonie Doon!
An' wha on Ayr your chanters tune!
Come, join the melancholious croon   dirge
O' Robin's reed!
His heart will never get aboon –
His Mailie's dead!

Tam o' Shanter

Written at Ellisland late in 1790, Burns describes 'Tam o' Shanter' as a tale, and it has that wonderful tall-story quality, which keeps the reader in suspense right until the end. It gathers momentum all the way through, from Tam's reluctant leave-taking of the seductive warmth of the tavern, until his breakneck escape over the bridge. The 'moral' of the tale brings the page to a halt with the warning:

> Whene'er to drink you are inclin'd,
> Or cutty sarks run in your mind,
> Think! ye may buy the joys o'er dear,
> Remember Tam o' Shanter's mare.

Jean Armour maintained her husband wrote the poem in a day as he walked by the river, laughing and crying with delight as he worked. But the idea could have come from an earlier period in his life, when he mixed with the Ayrshire farmers from Kirkoswald. It has been suggested that the inspiration for Tam was Douglas Graham of Shanter (a steading between Turnberry and Culzean) a farmer, who with his friend John Davidson, regularly visited the Ayr markets, often staying late in town drinking. Graham had a nagging wife, who warned him about his late night sojourns and it seems that after one of these binges, when he lost his bonnet containing all the day's takings, he made up a tale about witches in the Alloway Kirkyard. Another resident of Kirkoswald at that time was Katie Steven or Stein, a fortune-teller, also reputed to be a witch and seemingly the model for 'Cutty Sark'.

Promising to write a supernatural tale for Francis Grose to be included in the second volume of his *Antiquities of Scotland*, published in 1791, Burns's fertile imagination wove together old pieces of gossip, everyday superstitions and well-known stories of Alloway's haunted churchyard into an ever-popular 'ripping yarn'.

Tam o' Shanter

A Tale

'Of Brownyis and of Bogillis full is this Buke.'
GAWIN DOUGLAS

When chapman billies leave the street,   *packman fellows*
And drouthy neebors neebors meet;   *thirsty*
As market days are wearing late,
An' folk begin to tak the gate;   *road*
While we sit bousing at the nappy,   *ale*
An' gettin fou and unco happy,   *full, mellow – very*
We think na on the lang Scots miles,
The mosses, waters, slaps, and stiles,   *bogs – gaps*
That lie between us and our hame,
Whare sits our sulky sullen dame,
Gathering her brows like gathering storm,
Nursing her wrath to keep it warm.

This truth fand honest Tam o' Shanter,   *found*
As he frae Ayr ae night did canter:
(Auld Ayr, wham ne'er a town surpasses)
For honest men and bonny lasses).

O Tam! hadst thou but been sae wise
As taen thy ain wife Kate's advice!
She tauld thee weel thou was a skellum,   *rogue*
A blethering, blustering drunken blellum;
That frae November till October
Ae market-day thou was na sober;
That ilka melder wi' the miller   *every*
Thou sat as lang as thou had siller;   *money*
That every naig was ca'd a shoe on   *shod*
The smith and thee gat roaring fou on;
That at the L–d's house, ev'n on Sunday,
Thou drank wi' Kirkton Jean till Monday.
She prophesy'd that, late or soon,
Thou wad be found deep drown'd in Doon;
Or catch'd wi' warlocks in the mirk   *wizards – darkness*
By Alloway's auld haunted kirk.

63

Ah, gentle dames! it gars me greet   makes – weep
To think how mony counsels sweet,
How mony lengthen'd, sage advices
The husband from the wife despises!

But to our tale: – Ae market night,
Tam had got planted unco right;
Fast by an ingle, bleezing finely,   fire
Wi' reaming swats, that drank
   divinely;   foaming – new ale
And at his elbow, Souter Johnny,   Cobbler
His ancient, trusty, drouthy crony;   thirsty
Tam lo'ed him like a very brither;
Thay had been fou for weeks thegither.
The night drave on wi' sangs and clatter;
And ay the ale was growing better:
The Landlady and Tam grew gracious
Wi' favours secret, sweet and precious:
The Souter tauld his queerest stories;
The landlord's laugh was ready chorus:
The storm without might rair and rustle,   roar
Tam did na mind the storm a whistle.

Care, mad to see a man sae happy,
E'en drown'd himself amang the nappy;
As bees flee hame wi' lades o' treasure,   loads
The minutes wing'd their way wi' pleasure:
Kings may be blest, but Tam was glorious,
O'er a' the ills o' life victorious!

But pleasures are like poppies spread,
You seize the flow'r, its bloom is shed;
Or like the snow falls in the river,
A moment white – then melts for ever;
Or like the borealis race
That flit ere you can point their place;
Or like the rainbow's lovely form
Evanishing amid the storm.
Nae man can tether time or tide;
The hour approaches Tam maun ride;   must
That hour, o' night's black arch the key-stane,
That dreary hour he mounts his beast in;
And sic a night he taks the road in
As ne'er poor sinner was abroad in.

The wind blew as 'twad blawn its last; would have
The rattling show'rs rose on the blast;
The speedy gleams the darkness swallow'd;
Loud, deep, and lang, the thunder bellow'd:
That night a child might understand
The Deil had business on his hand.

Weel mounted on his gray mare, Meg,
A better never lifted leg,
Tam skelpit on thro' dub and mire, rattled – puddle
Despising wind, and rain, and fire;
Whiles holding fast his gude blue bonnet;
Whiles crooning o'er some auld Scots humming
    sonnet;
Whiles glow'ring round wi' prudent cares gazing
Lest bogles catch him unawares: hobgoblins
Kirk-Alloway was drawing nigh,
Whare ghaists and houlets nightly cry. owls

By this time he was 'cross the ford,
Whare in the snaw the chapman
    smoor'd; smothered
And past the birks and meikle stane birches – big
Whare drunken Charlie brak's neck-bane;
And thro' the whins, and by the gorse
    cairn pile of stones
Whare hunters fand the murder'd bairn; child
And near the thorn, aboon the well, above
Whare Mungo's mither hang'd hersel.
Before him Doon pours all his floods,
The doubling storm roars thro' the woods;
The lightnings flash frae pole to pole;
Near and more near the thunders roll:
When, glimmering thro' the groaning trees,
Kirk-Alloway seem'd in a bleeze;
Thro' ilka bore the beams were every cranny
    glancing;
And loud resounded mirth and dancing.

Inspiring bold John Barleycorn!
What dangers thou canst make us scorn!
Wi' tippenny we fear nae evil;
Wi' usquabae we'll face the devil!   whisky
The swats sae ream'd in Tammie's noddle,
Fair play, he car'd na deils a boddle.
But Maggie stood right sair astonish'd,
Till, by the heel and hand admonish'd,
She ventur'd forward on the light;
And, vow! Tam saw an unco   in sooth! – marvellous
   sight!

Warlocks and witches in a dance;
Nae cotillion brent new frae France,   brand-new
But hornpipes, jigs, strathspeys and reels,
Put life and mettle in their heels.
A winnock-bunker in the east,   window-recess
There sat auld Nick, in shape o' beast;
A towzie tyke, black, grim and large,   shaggy dog
To gie them music was his charge:
He screw'd the pipes and gart them   made
   skirl   scream
Till roof and rafters a' did dirl.   vibrate
Coffins stood round, like open presses, cupboards
That shaw'd the dead in their last dresses;
And, by some devilish cantraip sleight,   weird trick
Each in its cauld hand held a light –
By which heroic Tam was able
To note upon the haly table
A murderer's banes, in gibbet-airns;   irons
Twa span-lang, wee, unchristen'd bairns;
A thief new-cutted frae a rape,   from a rope
Wi' his last gasp his gab did gape;   mouth
Five tomahawks wi' blude red-rusted;
Five scymitars wi' murder crusted;
A garter which a babe had strangled;
A knife a father's throat had mangled –
Whom his ain son o' life bereft –
The grey hairs yet stack to the
   heft;   stuck to the handle
Wi' mair of horrible and awefu',
Which ev'n to name wad be unlawfu'.

As Tammie glowr'd, amaz'd and curious,   stared
The mirth and fun grew fast and furious:
The piper loud and louder blew,
The dancers quick and quicker flew:
They reel'd, they set, they cross'd, they
    cleekit,   took hands
Till ilka carlin swat and reekit,   witch – steamed
And coost her duddies to the   threw off – clothes
    wark,
And linket at it in her sark!   set to it – shift

Now Tam, O Tam! had thae been   these
    queans,   young women
A' plump and strapping in their teens!
Their sarks, instead o' creeshie
    flannen,   greasy flannel
Been snaw-white seventeen hunder linnen! –
Thir breeks o' mine, my only pair,   These
That ance were plush, o' gude blue hair,
I wad hae gi'en them off my hurdies   buttocks
For ae blink o' the bonie burdies!   birds

But wither'd beldams, auld and droll,
Rigwoodie hags wad spean a foal,
Lowping and flinging   Leaping
    on a crummock,   stick with a crooked head
I wonder didna turn thy stomach.

But Tam kend what was what fu' brawlie: quite well
There was ae winsome wench and wawlie,   comely
That night enlisted in the core   corps
(Lang after kend on Carrick shore:
For mony a beast to dead she shot,   death
And perish'd mony a bonny boat,
And shook baith meikle corn and bear,   much barley
And held the country-side in fear).
Her cutty sark, o' Paisley   short shift –
    harn,   coarse linen
That while a lassie she had worn,
In longitude tho' sorely scanty,
It was her best, and she was vauntie. –   proud of it

Ah! little kend thy reverend grannie,
That sark she coft for her wee Nannie,   bought
Wi' two pund Scots ('twas a' her   3s. 6d. English
    riches),
Wad ever grac'd a dance of witches!

But here my Muse her wing maun cour   fold
Sic flights are far beyond her pow'r;
To sing how Nannie lap and flang   leaped – kicked
(A souple jade she was and strang),
And how Tam stood like ane bewitch'd
And though his very een enrich'd;
Even Satan glowr'd, and fidg'd   gazed and
    fu' fain,   hitched his shoulders in glee
And hotch'd and blew wi' might and   squirmed
    main,
Till first ae caper, syne anither,   then
Tam tint his reason a' thegither   lost – altogether
And roars out 'Weel done, Cutty-sark!'
And in an instant all was dark;
And scarcely had he Maggie rallied,
When out the hellish legion sallied.

As bees bizz out wi' angry fyke,   fret
When plundering herds assail
    their byke;   herd-boys – nest
As open pussie's mortal foes,   the hare's
When, pop! she starts before their nose;
As eager runs the market-crowd,
When 'Catch the thief!' resounds aloud;
So Maggie runs – the witches follow,
Wi' mony an eldritch skreech and hollow. frightful

Ah, Tam! Ah, Tam! thou'll get thy
    fairin!   reward, treat
In hell they'll roast thee like a herrin!
In vain thy Kate awaits thy comin!
Kate soon will be a woefu' woman!
Now, do thy speedy utmost, Meg,
And win the key-stane of the brig;   reach
There, at them thou thy tail may toss:
A running stream they dare na cross.
But ere the key-stane she could make,
The fient a tail she had to shake!   No tail had she

68

For Nannie, far before the rest,
Hard upon noble Maggie prest,
And flew at Tam wi' furious ettle: endeavour
But little wist she Maggie's mettle –
Ae spring brought off her master hale,   whole
But left behind her ain grey tail:
The carlin claught her by the rump,   clutched
And left poor Maggie scarce a stump.

Now, wha this tale o' truth shall read,
Ilk man and mother's son, take heed:
Whene'er to drink you are inclin'd,
Or cutty sarks run in your mind,
Think! ye may buy the joys o'er dear,
Remember Tam o' Shanter's mare.

The Auld Farmer's New-Year Morning Salutation to his Auld Mare, Maggie

The farmer's salute to his mare as he feeds her the traditional New Year ripp of corn, is a sympathetic and gentle reminder of the affinity man has with the animals who share his burdens. He remembers his mare, now 'dowie, stiff an' crazy' when she was 'steeve an' swank'; as he recalls her youth, he recalls his own, bound together by toil and memories. Written in 1786 at Mossgiel, the poem is similar to 'John Anderson, my Jo' in its sentiment.

The Auld Farmer's New-Year Morning Salutation to his Auld Mare, Maggie

ON GIVING HER THE ACCUSTOMED RIPP OF CORN TO HANSEL IN THE NEW-YEAR

A guid New-year I wish thee, Maggie!	
Hae, there's a ripp to thy	handful
auld baggie:	stomach
Tho' thou's howe-backit now,	hollow-backed
an' knaggie,	bony
I've seen the day	
Thou could hae gaen like ony staggie,	colt
Out-owre the lay.	lea

Tho' now thou's dowie, stiff an' crazy,	drooping
An' thy auld hide as white 's a daisie,	
I've seen thee dappl't, sleek an' glaizie,	
A bonie gray:	
He should been tight that daur't to	dared
raize thee,	excite
Ance in a day.	

70

Thou ance was i' the foremost rank,
A filly buirdly, steeve an'
   swank;   strong – firm – stately
An' set weel down a shapely shank,
As e'er tread yird;   earth
An' could hae flown out-owre a stank,   ditch
Like ony bird.

It's now some nine-an'-twenty year,
Sin' thou was my guidfather's meere;   mare
He gied me thee, o' tocher clear,   gave – dowry
An' fifty mark;
Tho' it was sma', 'twas weel-won gear,   well-earned
An' thou was stark.   money

When first I gaed to woo my Jenny,
Ye then was trottin wi' your minnie: mother
Tho' ye was trickie, slee, an' funnie,   sly
Ye ne'er was donsie,   mischievous
But hamely, tawie, quiet, an' cannie,
An' unco sonsie   very plump

That day, ye pranc'd wi' muckle pride,   great
When ye bure hame my bonie bride: bore
An' sweet an' gracefu' she did ride,
Wi' maiden air!
Kyle-Stewart I could bragget   could have bragged,
   wide,   challenged
For sic a pair.

Tho' now ye dow but hoyte and hobble, can – limp
An' wintle like a saumont-coble, twist and rock –
               salmon-boat
That day, ye was a jinker noble,   runner
For heels an' win'!   wind
An' ran them till they a' did wauble, reel
Far, far behin'!

When thou an' I were young an'
   skiegh,   high-mettled
An' stable-meals at fairs were driegh,   tedious
How thou wad prance, an' snore, an'
   skriegh,   whinny
An' tak the road!
Town's bodies ran, an' stood abiegh, out of the way
An' ca't thee mad.   called

When thou was corn't, an'
   I was mellow,   *made comfortable*
                                      by drink
We took the road ay like a swallow:
At brooses thou had ne'er a fellow,
For pith an' speed;
But ev'ry tail thou pay't them hollow,
Whare'er thou gaed.

The sma', droop-rumpl't,   *drooping at the crupper*
   hunter cattle
Might aiblins waur't thee for a brattle; *perhaps beat –*
                                    short race
But sax Scotch mile, thou try't their mettle,   *six*
An' gar't them whaizle: *made – wheeze*
Nae whip nor spur, but just a wattle   *switch*
O' saugh or hazle.   *willow*

Thou was a noble 'fittie-lan','
As e'er in tug or tow was drawn!
Aft thee an' I, in aught hours' gaun, *eight hours' work*
On guid March-weather,
Hae turn'd sax rood beside our han',   *six roods*
For days thegither.

Thou never braing't, an'
   fetch't, an' flisket;   *fretted – raged – kicked*
But thy auld tail thou wad hae whisket,   *lashed*
An' spread abreed thy weel-fill'd brisket,   *breast*
Wi' pith an' power;
Till sprittie knowes wad rair't an' risket,
An' slypet owre.

When frosts lay lang, an' snaws were deep,   *long*
An' threaten'd labour back to keep,
I gied thy cog a wee bit heap
Aboon the timmer:
I ken'd my Maggie wad na sleep
For that, or simmer.   *before summer*

In cart or car thou never reestet;   *stood still*
The steyest brae thou wad hae fac't it; *steepest hill*
Thou never lap, an' stenned, an'   *leaped – reared*
   breastet,
Then stood to blaw;
But just thy step a wee thing hastet, *a little – quickened*
Thou snoov't awa.   *pushed on quietly*

My 'pleugh' is now thy bairn-time a',
Four gallant brutes as e'er did draw;
Forbye sax mae I've sell't awa,   *Besides six more*
That thou has nurst:
They drew me thretteen pund an' twa   *thirteen*
The vera warst.

Mony a sair daurg we twa hae wrought,   *day's work*
An' wi' the weary warl' fought!   *world*
An' mony an anxious day, I thought
We wad be beat!
Yet here to crazy age we're brought,
Wi' something yet.

An' think na', my auld trusty servan',
That now perhaps thou's less deservin,
An' thy auld days may end in starvin,
For my last fow,   *bushel*
A heapet stimpart, I'll reserve ane
Laid by for you.

We've worn to crazy years thegither;
We'll toyte about wi' ane anither;   *move*
Wi' tentie care I'll flit thy tether   *heedful*
To some hain'd rig,   *reserved piece of ground*
Whare ye may nobly rax your leather,   *stretch*
Wi' sma fatigue.

The Banks o' Doon

Born in 1768, Peggy Kennedy was the daughter of Robert Kennedy of Daljarroch and a niece of the poet's friend Gavin Hamilton. Burns first met her in Mauchline in 1785, when she was staying with the Hamiltons and as a compliment to her beauty he wrote the song 'Young Peggy' and sent it to her. In the accompanying letter he wished her good fortune and hoped that 'the snares of villainy may never beset you in the road of life.' It would appear he was almost prophetic in his desire for her protection. This much better known, later song laments the treachery she indeed found with her 'fause luver'.

By the time Peggy met Burns she was already involved with Captain Andrew McDowall of Logan, who at the age of only twenty-five was MP for Wigton. They became engaged and were subsequently married by a 'secret ceremony' arranged by McDowall. When a daughter was

born in 1794, just as he inherited his father's estates, he had the marriage declared void and promptly married the daughter of a Dumfriesshire laird, considering the alliance more propitious. In 1795 Peggy brought a court action to have the marriage recognized and her daughter declared legitimate, but she died before a decision was reached. By 1798 the Constitutional Court of the Church declared the marriage legal, but McDowall had that verdict overturned in the Court of Session. The only proviso was an award of £3000 to her daughter for the distress suffered by her mother.

The Banks o' Doon

TUNE – *Caledonian Hunt's Delight*

Ye banks and braes o' bonie Doon,
How can ye bloom sae fresh and fair!
How can ye chant, ye little birds,
And I sae weary fu' o' care!
Thou'll break my heart, thou warbling bird
That wantons thro' the flowering thorn:
Thou minds me o' departed joys,
Departed, never to return.

Aft hae I rov'd by bonie Doon,
To see the rose and woodbine twine;
And ilka bird sang o' its luve,   every
And fondly sae did I o' mine;
Wi' lightsome heart I pu'd a rose,
Fu' sweet upon its thorny tree;
And my fause luver staw my rose,   false
But, ah! he left the thorn wi' me.

The Cotter's Saturday Night

For a poet, such as Burns, who wrote baldly and vigorously about man's pains and pleasures, this idyllic portrait of a rural family as they gather at their cottage on a Saturday night seems cumbersome and lacking in reality. He was too close, and trying too hard to say too much about what he saw as the hitherto unsung, sterling qualities of the average Scottish labouring family. It was written a year after his father's death, in 1785, and there is little doubt that the father in the poem is William Burnes.

We can see that the constant switch in the language from English to Scots creates a falseness. But it also reveals a problem of many Scots at that time, who, whilst thinking and speaking in their native tongue, were forced to use English on formal occasions and during religious worship. The use of both languages also highlights the duality and displacement felt by a people forced to relinquish their own government. But the poem makes the statement, and this is what Burns was trying so desperately to put across, that no matter what the circumstances, the solid, reliable Scottish peasant family still clung to and gained strength from the traditional values of the Bible, the family and a loyalty to the country of its birth.

The Cotter's Saturday Night

INSCRIBED TO R. AIKEN, ESQ

Let not Ambition mock their useful toil,
Their homely joys, and destiny obscure;
Nor Grandeur hear, with a disdainful smile,
The short and simple annals of the poor. – GRAY

My lov'd, my honor'd, much respected friend!
No mercenary bard his homage pays;
With honest pride, I scorn each selfish end,
My dearest meed, a friend's esteem and praise:
To you I sing, in simple Scottish lays,
The lowly train in life's sequester'd scene;
The native feelings strong, the guileless ways;
What Aiken in a cottage would have been;
Ah! tho' his worth unknown, far happier there I
    ween!

November chill blaws loud wi'
    angry sugh;   whistling sound
The short'ning winter-day is near a close;
The miry beasts retreating frae the pleugh;
The black'ning trains o' craws to their   crows
    repose:
The toil-worn Cotter frae his labor goes, –
This night his weekly moil is at an end,
Collects his spades, his mattocks, and his hoes,
Hoping the morn in ease and rest to spend,
And weary, o'er the moor, his course does
    hameward bend.

At length his lonely cot appears in view,
Beneath the shelter of an aged tree;
Th' expectant wee-things, toddlin, stacher stagger
    through
To meet their 'dad,' wi' flichterin' noise   fluttering
    and glee.
His wee bit ingle blinking bonilie,
His clean hearth-stane, his thrifty wifie's smile,
The lisping infant, prattling on his knee,
Does a' his weary kiaugh and care beguile, anxiety
And make him quite forget his labor and his toil.

77

Belyve, the elder bairns come drappin in, By-and-by
At service out, amang the farmers roun';
Some ca' the pleugh, some herd, some
    tentie rin   attentively
A cannie errand to a neibor town;   private
Their eldest hope, their Jenny, woman-grown,
In youthfu' bloom – love sparkling in her e'e –
Comes hame; perhaps, to shew a braw new gown,
Or deposite her sair-won
    penny-fee,   hard-earned wages
To help her parents dear, if they in hardship be.

With joy unfeign'd, brothers and sisters meet,
And each for other's welfare kindly spiers: inquires
The social hours, swift-wing'd, unnotic'd fleet;
Each tells the uncos that he sees or hears.   news
The parents partial eye their hopeful years;
Anticipation forward points the view;
The mother, wi' her needle and her sheers,
Gars auld claes look amaist as   Makes – clothes
    weel's the new;
The father mixes a' wi' admonition due.

Their master's and their mistress's command,
The younkers a' are warnèd to obey;
And mind their labors wi' an eydent hand, diligent
And ne'er, tho' out o' sight, to jauk or play;   dally
'And O! be sure to fear the Lord alway,
And mind your duty, duly, morn and night;
Lest in temptation's path ye gang astray,
Implore His counsel and assisting might:
They never sought in vain that sought the Lord
    aright!'

But hark! a rap comes gently to the door;
Jenny, wha kens the meaning o' the same,
Tells how a neibor lad came o'er the moor,
To do some errands, and convoy her hame.
The wily mother sees the conscious flame
Sparkle in Jenny's e'e, and flush her cheek;
With heart-struck anxious care, enquires his
   name,
While Jenny hafflins is afraid to speak;   *almost*
Weel-pleas'd the mother hears, it's nae wild,
   worthless rake.

Wi' kindly welcome, Jenny brings him ben;
A strappin' youth, he takes the mother's eye;
Blythe Jenny sees the visit's no ill ta'en;   *received*
The father cracks of horses, pleughs, and kye.
The youngster's artless heart o'erflows wi' joy,
But blate an' laithfu', scarce can   *bashful – hesitating*
   weel behave;
The mother, wi' a woman's wiles, can spy
What makes the youth sae bashfu' and sae grave;
Weel-pleas'd to think her bairn's respected   *child*
   like the lave.   *rest*

O happy love! where love like this is found:
O heart-felt raptures! bliss beyond compare!
I've pacèd much this weary, mortal round,
And sage experience bids me this declare, –
'If Heaven a draught of heavenly pleasure spare –
One cordial in this melancholy vale,
'Tis when a youthful, loving, modest pair
In other's arms, breathe out the tender tale,
Beneath the milk-white thorn that scents the
   evening gale.'

Is there, in human form, that bears a heart,
A wretch! a villain! lost to love and truth!
That can, with studied, sly, ensnaring art,
Betray sweet Jenny's unsuspecting youth?
Curse on his perjur'd arts! dissembling, smooth!
Are honor, virtue, conscience, all exil'd?
Is there no pity, no relenting ruth,
Points to the parents fondling o'er their child?
Then paints the ruin'd maid, and their distraction
   wild?

But now the supper crowns their simple board,
The halesome parritch, chief of Scotia's
    food;   porridge
The sowpe their only hawkie does   food – cow
    afford,
That, 'yont the hallan snugly chows her   porch
    cood: cud
The dame brings forth, in complimental mood,
To grace the lad, her weel-hain'd kebbuck,
    fell;   well-matured cheese, tasty
And aft he's prest, and aft he ca's it guid;
The frugal wifie, garrulous, will tell
How 'twas a towmond auld, sin' lint was
    i' the bell.   twelvemonth – flax in flower

The cheerfu' supper done, wi' serious face,
They, round the ingle, form a circle wide;
The sire turns o'er, with patriarchal grace,
The big ha'-bible, ance his father's   large Bible,
    pride: that lay in the hall
His bonnet rev'rently is laid aside,
His lyart haffets wearing thin and bare; grey side-locks
Those strains that once did sweet in Zion glide,
He wales a portion with judicious care;   selects
And 'Let us worship God!' he says with solemn air.

They chant their artless notes in simple guise,
They tune their hearts, by far the noblest aim;
Perhaps 'Dundee's' wild-warbling measures rise,
Or plaintive 'Martyrs,' worthy of the name;
Or noble 'Elgin' beets the heaven-ward flame, fans
The sweetest far of Scotia's holy lays:
Compar'd with these, Italian trills are tame;
The tickl'd ears no heart-felt raptures raise;
Nae unison hae they, with our Creator's praise.

The priest-like father reads the sacred page,
How Abram was the friend of God on high;
Or, Moses bade eternal warfare wage
With Amalek's ungracious progeny;
Or, how the royal bard did groaning lie
Beneath the stroke of Heaven's avenging ire;
Or Job's pathetic plaint, and wailing cry;
Or rapt Isaiah's wild, seraphic fire;
Or other holy seers that tune the sacred lyre.

Perhaps the Christian volume is the theme,
How guiltless blood for guilty man was shed;
How He, who bore in Heaven the second name,
Had not on earth whereon to lay His head:
How His first followers and servants sped;
The precepts sage they wrote to many a land:
How he, who lone in Patmos banishèd,
Saw in the sun a mighty angel stand,
And heard great Bab'lon's doom pronounc'd by
    Heaven's command.

Then kneeling down to Heaven's Eternal King,
The saint, the father, and the husband prays:
Hope 'springs exulting on triumphant wing,'
That thus they all shall meet in future days,
There, ever bask in uncreated rays,
No more to sigh, or shed the bitter tear,
Together hymning their Creator's praise,
In such society, yet still more dear;
While circling Time moves round in an eternal
    sphere.

Compar'd with this, how poor Religion's pride,
In all the pomp of method, and of art;
When men display to congregations wide
Devotion's ev'ry grace, except the heart!
The Power, incens'd, the pageant will desert,
The pompous strain, the sacerdotal stole;
But haply, in some cottage far apart,
May hear, well pleas'd, the language of the soul;
And in His Book of Life the inmates poor enroll.

Then homeward all take off their sev'ral way;
The youngling cottagers retire to rest: youthful
The parent-pair their secret homage pay,
And proffer up to Heaven the warm request,
That He who stills the raven's cam'rous nest,
And decks the lily fair in flow'ry pride,
Would, in the way His wisdom sees the best,
For them and for their little ones provide;
But chiefly, in their hearts with grace divine
    preside.

From scenes like these, old Scotia's grandeur
    springs,
That makes her lov'd at home, rever'd abroad:
Princes and lords are but the breath of kings,
'An honest man's the noblest work of God;'
And certes, in fair virtue's heavenly road,
The cottage leaves the place far behind;
What is a lordling's pomp? – a cumbrous load,
Disguising oft the wretch of human kind,
Studied in arts of hell, in wickedness refin'd!

O Scotia! my dear, my native soil!
For whom my warmest wish to Heaven is sent,
Long may thy hardy sons of rustic toil
Be blest with health, and peace, and sweet
    content!
And O! may Heaven their simple lives prevent
From luxury's contagion, weak and vile!
Then, howe'er crowns and coronets be rent,
A virtuous populace may rise the while,
And stand a wall of fire around their much-lov'd
    isle.

O Thou! who pour'd the patriotic tide,
That stream'd thro' Wallace's undaunted heart,
Who dar'd to, nobly, stem tyrannic pride,
Or nobly die, the second glorious part:
(The patriot's God, peculiarly thou art,
His friend, inspirer, guardian, and reward!)
O never, never, Scotia's realm desert;
But still the patriot, and the patriot-bard,
In bright succession raise, her ornament and
   guard!

The Deil's awa wi' th' Exciseman

Several ideas have been mooted as to where and when this humorous song originated. It was written during the Dumfries years, around 1792, when Burns was making a living purely as an exciseman, having given up the lease on Ellisland farm. In the original story Burns was said to have composed the piece as he waited with his men on the Solway shore, before boarding the French ship *Rosamond* and impounding her cargo. The other officer Lewars, sent to Dumfries for reinforcements, took so long to return that the men became irritated and began to complain about his tardiness, one suggesting that 'the devil take him for his pains.' After this remark Burns wandered along the salt marches alone, and returned to sing them this song. But Burns's own account would seem to refute this as he always said he wrote it on the back of a letter during an excise court dinner, before passing it to the chairman to read aloud.

Another version told by Frank Miller of Annan in 1890 maintains the song was first delivered in front of a large audience in a house in the High Street of Annan.

Robert Chambers's hypothesis, that the song was first inspired by a similar work of Northumbrian poet Thomas Whittell and that Burns, with this in mind, composed his own version while walking on the Solway beach, delivering the completed song at the excise dinner and at a party in Annan, would seem to tie all the differing accounts together.

The Deil's awa wi' th' Exciseman

Tune – *The Looking-glass*

The deil cam fiddlin thro' the town,
And danc'd awa wi' th' Exciseman;
And ilka wife cries 'Auld Mahoun,   *every*
I wish you luck o' the prize, man.'

Chorus – The deil's awa, the deil's awa,
          The deil's awa wi' th' Exciseman,
          He's danc'd awa, he's danc'd awa,
          He's danc'd awa wi' th' Exciseman.

We'll make our maut and we'll brew our drink,
We'll laugh, sing and rejoice, man!
And mony braw thanks to the meikle   *hearty –*
   black deil   *big*
That danc'd awa wi' th' Exciseman.

There's threesome reels, there's foursome reels,
There's hornpipes and strathspeys, man,
But the ae best dance e'er cam to the Land
Was 'The deil's awa wi' th' Exciseman.'

The Holy Fair

Burns's title sums up the contrasting qualities in this old rural custom of celebrating communion *en masse*. 'Occasions', as they were called, were held in many different districts once a year, each parish and its minister joining up with others to form a large congregation. Each minister preached and here Burns describes in detail their individual styles and peculiarities, making them instantly recognizable in Ayrshire at that time. Because of the mass congregations the churches were often too small, the services being held in an adjoining field, where the 'Holy Fair' disintegrated into a fair.

An excuse for young men and women to meet and old friends to catch up with gossip, the Holy Fair had the air of a large celebration, not necessarily a religious one. As the ministers droned on, some slept in the field, others ate or sat round the beer barrels drinking until evening, when they descended on the local taverns.

Burns illuminates the gap between the supposed piety of the occasion and the actual fun of the fair, but his humour is of the Chaucerian variety, joyous and mocking, not the bitter satire of 'Holy Willie's Prayer'. His attacks on Calvinism came in many guises but his simple phrase that it was 'inappropriate to people' seems manifest here in this topsy-turvy religious fairground, where human instincts inevitably triumph over soul-destroying hypocrisy.

Probably written in 1785 after the Mauchline Communion held on the second Sunday in August, the poem was revised and completed in the spring of 1786.

The Holy Fair

A robe of seeming truth and trust
Hid crafty observation;
And secret hung, with poison'd crust,
The dirk of defamation:
A mask that like the gorget show'd,
Dye-varying on the pigeon;
And for a mantle large and broad,
He wrapt him in *Religion*.

Hypocrisy à-la-Mode

Upon a simmer Sunday morn,   summer
When Nature's face is fair,
I walkèd forth to view the corn,
An' snuff the caller air.   fresh
The rising sun owre Galston muirs   over
Wi' glorious light was glintin;
The hares were hirplin down the furrs,   creeping –
                                        furrows
The lav'rocks they were chantin   larks
Fu' sweet that day.

As lightsomely I glowr'd abroad,   with light heart –
                                        gazed
To see a scene sae gay,
Three hizzies, early at the road,   wenches
Cam skelpin up the way.   hurrying, walking smartly
Twa had manteeles o' dolefu' black,   mantles
But ane wi' lyart lining;   grey
The third, that gaed a-wee a-back,   held a little aloof
Was in the fashion shining,
Fu' braw that day.   very elegant

The *twa* appear'd like sisters twin,
In feature, form an' claes;
Their visage wither'd, lang an' thin,
An, sour as ony slaes: sloes
The *third* cam up,
    hap-step-an'-lowp   hop-step-and-leap
As light as ony lambie,
An' wi' a curchie low did stoop,   courtesy
As soon as e'er she saw me,
Fu' kind that day.

Wi' bonnet aff, quoth I, 'Sweet lass,
I think ye seem to ken me;   know
I'm sure I've seen that bonie face,
But yet I canna name ye,'   cannot
Quo' she, an' laughin as she spak,
An' taks me by the hands,
'Ye, for my sake, hae gien the feck   bulk
Of a' the ten commands   commandments
A screed some day.   rent

'My name is Fun – your cronie dear,
The nearest friend ye hae;
An' this is Superstition here,
An' that's Hypocrisy.
I'm gaun to Mauchline "Holy fair,"   going
To spend an hour in daffin: sport
Gin ye'll go there, yon runkl'd pair,   If – wrinkled
We will get famous laughin
At them this day.'

Quoth I, 'With a' my heart, I'll do'
I'll get my Sunday's sark on,   shirt
An' meet you on the holy spot;
Faith, we 'se hae fine remarkin!'
Then I gaed hame at   went –
    crowdie-time,   breakfast-time
An' soon I made me ready;
For roads were clad, from side to side,   filled
Wi' monie a wearie body,   many
In droves that day.

Here farmers gash, in ridin graith,   sensible – attire
Gaed hoddin by their cotters;   jogging beside
There swankies young,   strapping fellows
    in braw braid-claith,   fine broadcloth
Are springin owre the gutters.
The lasses, skelpin barefit,   hastening barefooted
    thrang,   crowded together
In silks an' scarlets glitter;
Wi' sweet-milk cheese, in monie a
    whang,   large piece
An' farls bak'd wi' butter,   cakes
Fu' crump that day.   hard and brittle

87

When by the 'plate' we set our nose,   *plate for the 'collection' or offertory*
Weel heapèd up wi ha'pence,
A greedy glowr 'black-bonnet' throws   *stare*
An' we maun draw our tippence.   *must bring out – twopence*
Then in we go to see the show,
On ev'ry side they're gathrin;
Some carryin dails, some chairs an' stools,   *deals*
An' some are busy blethrin   *gossiping*
Right loud that day.

Here stands a shed to fend the show'rs,   *ward off*
An' screen our countra gentry;
There 'Racer Jess,' an' twa-three w–s,
Are blinkin at the entry.
Here sits a raw o' tittlin jads,   *giggling girls*
Wi heavin breasts an' bare neck;
An' there a batch o' wabster lads   *group – weaver*
Blackguarding frae Kilmarnock,   *Come bent on mischief*
For fun this day.

Here some are thinkin on their sins,
An' some upo' their claes;   *upon – clothes*
Ane curses feet that fyl'd his shins   *one – defiled*
Anither sighs an' prays: *another*
On this hand sits a chosen swatch,   *sample*
Wi' screw'd-up, grace-proud faces;
On that a set o' chaps, at watch,
Thrang winkin on the lasses   *Busy*
To chairs that day.

O happy is that man, an' blest!
Nae wonder that it pride him!
Whase ain dear lass, that he likes best,   *own*
Comes clinkin down beside him!   *sits down hastily*
Wi' arm repos'd on the chair back,
He sweetly does compose him;
Which, by degrees, slips round her neck,
An 's loof upon her bosom   *hand*
Unkend that day.   *unnoticed*

Now a' the congregation o'er
Is silent expectation;
For Moodie speels the holy door,   climbs
Wi' tidings o' dam–ation.
Should *Hornie*, as in ancient days,   Satan
'Mang sons o' God present him,
The vera sight o' Moodie's face,
To 's ain het hame had sent him   hot
Wi' fright that day.

Hear how he clears the points o' Faith
Wi' rattlin' an' thumpin!
Now meekly calm, now wild in wrath,
He's stampin, an' he's jumpin!
His lengthen'd chin, his turn'd-up snount,
His eldritch squeel an' gestures,   unearthly squeal
O how they fire the heart devout,
Like cantharidian plaisters   plasters of cantharides, used to produce blisters
On sic a day!

But hark! the tent has chang'd its voice;
There's peace an' rest nae langer;
For a' the real judges rise,
They canna sit for anger.
Smith opens out his cauld harangues,
On practice and on morals;
An' aff the godly pour in thrangs,   crowds
To gie the jar an' barrels
A lift that day.

What signifies his barren shine,
Of moral pow'rs an' reason?
His English style, an' gesture fine,
Are a' clean out o' season.
Like Socrates or Antonine,   Marcus Aurelius Antoninus
Or some auld pagan heathen,
The *moral man* he does define,
But ne'er a word o' *faith* in
That's right that day.

In guid time comes an antidote
Against sic poison'd nostrum;
For Peebles, frae the water-fit,
Ascends the holy rostrum:
See, up he's got the Word o' God,
An' meek an' mim has view'd it,   *primly*
While 'Common-sense' has taen the road,
An' aff, an' up the Cowgate
Fast, fast that day.

Wee Miller niest, the Guard relieves,   *next*
An' Orthodoxy raibles,   *rattles out*
Tho' in his heart he weel believes,
An' thinks it auld wives' fables:
But faith! the birkie wants a manse,   *fellow*
So, cannilie he hums them;
Altho' his carnal wit an' sense
Like hafflins-wise o'ercomes him   *partly*
At times that day.

Now, butt an' ben, the change-
    house fills,   *public-house*
Wi' yill-caup commentators;   *ale-cup*
Here's crying out for bakes an' gills,   *biscuits*
An' there the pint-stowp clatters;   *pint-measure*
While thick an' thrang, an' loud an' lang, *crowded*
Wi' Logic an' wi' Scripture,
They raise a din, that, in the end,
Is like to breed a rupture
O' wrath that day.

Leeze me on drink! it gies us mair   *Commend me to*
Than either school or college;
It kindles wit, it waukens lear,   *rouses – learning*
It pangs us fou o'knowledge   *crams – full*
Be 't whisky-gill or penny-wheep,   *very small beer*
Or ony stronger potion,
It never fails, on drinking deep,
To kittle up our notion,   *enliven our wits*
By night or day.

The lads an' lasses, blythely bent
To mind baith saul an' body, *both soul*
Sit round the table, weel content,
An' steer about the toddy. *stir*
On this ane's dress, an' that ane's leuk, *look*
They're making observations;
While some are cozie i' the neuk, *corner*
An' forming assignations.
  To meet some day.

But now the L–'s ain trumpet touts, *sounds*
Till a' the hills are rairin, *roaring with the echo*
And echoes back-return the shouts;
Black Russell is na spairin: *sparing*
His piercing words, like Highlan swords,
Divide the joints an' marrow;
His talk o' H–ll, whare devils dwell,
Our vera 'sauls does harrow'
  Wi' fright that day.

A vast, unbottom'd, boundless pit,
Fill'd fou o' lowin brunstane, *flaming brimstone*
Whase ragin flame, an' scorchin heat,
Wad melt the hardest whun-stane! *whinstone*
The half-asleep start up wi' fear,
An' think they hear it roarin,
When presently it does appear,
'Twas but some neebor snorin
  Asleep that day.

'Twad be owre lang a tale to tell *too long*
How monie stories past,
An' how they crouded to the yill, *ale*
When they were a' dismist:
How drink gaed round,
 in cogs an' caups *wooden dishes of different kinds*
Amang the furms an' benches;
An' cheese an' bread, frae women's laps,
Was dealt about in lunches, *large pieces*
  An' dawds that day. *lumps*

In comes a gawsie, gash   *buxom – sagacious*
  Guidwife,
An' sits down by the fire,
Syne draws her kebbuck an' her   *Then – cheese*
  knife,
The lasses they are shyer.
The auld Guidmen, about the *grace,*
Frae side to side they bother,
Till some ane by his bonnet lays,
An' gi'es them 't like a tether,   *gives it out as if*
                                   it were a rope
Fu' lang that day.

Waesucks! for him that gets nae lass,   *Alas!*
Or lasses that hae naething!
Sma' need has he to say a grace,
Or melvie his braw claithing!   *soil with meal –*
                                     fine clothes
O Wives be mindfu', ance yoursel
How bonie lads ye wanted,
An' dinna, for a kebbuck-heel,   *end of a cheese*
Let lasses be affronted
On sic a day!

Now 'Clinkumbell,' wi' rattlin tow,   *rope*
Begins to jow an' croon;   *peal – moan*
Some swagger hame the best they dow,   *can*
Some wait the afternoon.
At slaps the billies halt a blink,   *gaps in fences or walls –*
Till lasses strip their shoon: *young men – a short time*
                                    take off – shoes
Wi' faith an hope, an' love an' drink,
They're a' in famous tune
For crack that day.   *talk*

How monie hearts this day converts
O' Sinners and o' Lassies!
Their hearts o' stane, gin night, are gane   *before*
As saft as only flesh is.
There's some are fou o' love divine;
There's some are fou o' brandy;
An' monie jobs that day begin,
May end in Houghmagandie   *fornication*
Some ither day.

The Last Time I came o'er the Moor

Maria Riddell first met Burns in 1791 when she and her husband Walter returned from the West Indies to settle in Scotland. Walter was the younger brother of Captain Robert Riddell, Burns's friend and neighbour at Friars' Carse. The poet was taken with this flirtatious, talented beauty of nineteen and when she moved into Woodley Park near Dumfries, one year later, he became a frequent visitor. Impressed by her writing ability, he introduced her to his old friend William Smellie, a printer in Edinburgh, with the intention of having her work published. She played an important part in Burns's later life; often he enclosed poems and songs in his letters to her, asking for her opinion. But judging from the words of this song it was not only her intellect that stirred him. We do not have to search far for the 'guilty lover'. He sent the song to Maria saying the original name had been Mary, but that he changed it to Maria in her honour.

A, now infamous, incident in Robert Riddell's home at Christmas in 1793 soured their friendship for a time. After a large dinner party, the men, suffering from the effects of too much alcohol, decided as a joke to act out the rape of the Sabine women. Burns, egged on by the others, acted out his part with too much enthusiasm. Whether his prey was Robert's wife Elizabeth or Maria, it has never been made clear, but he was thrown out of the house and Maria advised to sever all connections with him. The following morning he wrote the well-known 'letter from Hell' to Elizabeth Riddell, pleading that the drink had been forced upon him by her husband and begging her forgiveness. It had no effect. The family rejected him; not really being part of their society, he was expendable.

Humiliated and bitter, Burns composed several unflattering portraits about Maria, even attaching one to her carriage. In spite of this, it was Maria who early in 1795 took the first step to heal the breach between them, sending him a book on the pretext that he 'had' to read it. After a cold, but courteous reply their letters soon returned to their former intimate, flirtatious tone. They last met at the Brow Well on the Solway on 5 July 1796. Burns knew he was dying and greeted her with 'Well, madam, have you any commands for the other world?'

The Last Time I came o'er the Moor

The last time I came o'er the moor,
And left Maria's dwelling,
What throes, what tortures passing cure,
Were in my bosom swelling:
Condemned to see my rival's reign,
While I in secret languish;
To feel a fire in every vein,
Yet dare not speak my anguish.

Love's veriest wretch, despairing, I
Fain, fain my crime would cover:
The unweeting groan, the bursting sigh,   unwitting
Betray the guilty lover.
I know my doom must be despair:
Thou wilt nor canst relieve me;
But, O Maria, hear my prayer,
For pity's sake, forgive me!

The music of thy tongue I heard,
Nor wist while it enslaved me;
I saw thine eyes, yet nothing feared,
Till fears no more had saved me.
The unwary sailor thus, aghast,
The wheeling torrent viewing,
Mid circling horrors yields at last
In overwhelming ruin!

The Rigs o' Barley

This joyous, suggestive celebration of midsummer and youth was written in the early years at Lochlie farm. Looking back on his work, Burns believed that last verse to be one of the finest he had written. Anne Rankine, the daughter of his friend and neighbour at the adjoining Adamhill farm always maintained she was the Annie of 'The Rigs o' Barley'. Her father was a well-known wag with a dislike of the clergy, he and the poet had much in common and remained friends for many years. Later, in *Epistle to John Rankine,* Burns described him as 'rough, rude ready-witted Rankine'.

The Rigs o' Barley

TUNE – *Corn Rigs*

Chorus – Corn rigs, an' barley rigs,
           An' corn rigs are bonie:
           I'll ne'er forget that happy night,
           Amang the rigs wi' Annie.

It was upon a Lammas night,
When corn rigs are bonie,
Beneath the moon's unclouded light,
I held awa to Annie;
The time flew by, wi' tentless heed,
Till 'tween the late and early,
Wi' sma' persuasion she agreed
To see me thro' the barley.

The sky was blue, the wind was still,
The moon was shining clearly;
I set her down, wi' right good will,
Amang the rigs o' barley:
I ken't her heart was a' my ain;
I lov'd her most sincerely;
I kiss'd her owre and owre again,
Amang the rigs o' barley.

I lock'd her in my fond embrace;
Her heart was beating rarely:
My blessings on that happy place,
Amang the rigs o' barley!
But by the moon and stars so bright,
That shone that hour so clearly!
She ay shall bless that happy night
Amang the rigs o' barley.

I hae been blythe wi' comrades dear;
I hae been merry drinking;
I hae been joyfu' gath'rin gear;
I hae been happy thinking:
But a' the pleasures e'er I saw,
Tho' three times doubl'd fairly –
That happy night was worth them a'
Amang the rigs o' barley.

The Selkirk Grace

During his tour of Galloway in 1794 Burns and his friend John Syme stayed for a few days with the Earl of Selkirk at St Mary's Isle, Kirkcudbright, the Selkirks' family home. The visit was a huge success with Burns at his very best, impressing his host and the other guests with his erudite wit and stimulating conversation. When asked to say the blessing before dinner he recited an old Scots grace, which thereafter became known as 'The Selkirk Grace'.

The Selkirk Grace

Some hae meat and canna eat,
And some wad eat that want it: would
But we hae meat and we can eat,
Sae let the Lord be thankit.

The Twa Dogs

Burns completed this satire in 1786 at Mossgiel, but it is a hangover from earlier days at Mount Oliphant, where the family lived in constant fear of the factor and his threats to evict them and seize their tools and cattle, because of rent arrears. It was due to this that his outrage at social injustice and his deep feelings of insecurity never left him. Here he depicts the vulnerability of a peasant class who, through ignorance, believe that the rich have cares greater than their own.

The work is part of a long Scottish tradition of animal poems, but Burns made his animals talk, or rather discuss the differences between the lives and attitudes of the rich and poor. Luath, the collie, the ploughman's dog, has a naivety bred through lack of knowledge, whereas Caesar, who has witnessed only lack in human terms, in the life of the rich, sees the world through cynical eyes. After exploring men's different lots, they leave one another relieved they are 'na men, but dogs'.

The poet's dog Luath was killed during an incident at Mount Oliphant the night before Burns's father died. Determined to immortalize his friend in print, he quite naturally became the ploughman's dog in this satiric swipe at the landed classes.

The Twa Dogs

A TALE

'Twas in that place o' Scotland's isle,
That bears the name o' auld 'King Coil,'
Upon a bonie day in June,
When wearing thro' the afternoon,
Twa dogs, that were na thrang at hame,   busy
Forgather'd ance upon a time.   Met together

The first I'll name, they ca'd him 'Caesar,'
Was keepet for his Honor's pleasure:
His hair, his size, his mouth, his lugs,   ears
Shew'd he was nane o' Scotland's dogs;
But whalpet some place far abroad,   whelped
Whare sailors gang to fish for cod.   *i.e.* Newfoundland

His lockèd, letter'd, braw brass-collar
Shew'd him the gentleman an' scholar;
But though he was o' high degree,
The fient a pride, nae pride   not the least pride
  had he;
But wad hae spent an hour caressin,
Ev'n wi' a tinkler-gipsey's messan: cur
At kirk or market, mill or smiddie,   smithy
Nae tawted tyke, tho' e'er   matted-haired dog
  sae duddie,   unkempt
But he wad stand, as glad to see him,
An' stroan'd on stanes an' hillocks wi' him.   stones

The tither was a ploughman's collie –   other
A rhyming, ranting, raving billie,   fellow
Wha for his friend an' comrade had him,
And in his freaks had 'Luath' ca'd him,
After some dog in Highland sang,
Was made lang syne – Lord knows how lang.

He was a gash an' faithfu' tyke,   *wise*
As ever lap a sheugh or dyke.   *leaped – ditch or wall*
His honest, sonsie, baws'nt face   *handsome*
Ay gat him friends in ilka place;   *every*
His breast was white, his tousie back   *shaggy*
Weel clad wi' coat o' glossy black;
His gawsie tail, wi' upward curl,   *handsome*
Hung owre his hurdies wi' a swirl.   *hips*

Nae doubt but they were fain o' ither,   *fond*
And unco pack an' thick thegither   *very intimate*
Wi' social nose whyles snuff'd an'
   snowket;   *sometimes – scented*
Whyles mice an' moudieworts they   *moles*
   howket;   *dug up*
Whyles scour'd awa' in lang excursion,
An' worry'd ither in diversion;   *each other*
Till tir'd at last wi' mony a farce,
They set them down upon their ——,
An' there began a lang digression
About the 'lords o' the creation.'

CAESAR

I've aften wonder'd, honest Luath,
What sort o' life poor dogs like you have;
An' when the gentry's life I saw,
What way poor bodies liv'd ava.   *at all*

Our laird gets in his rackèd rents,
His coals, his kane, an' a' his stents:
He rises when he likes himsel;
His flunkies answer at the bell;
He ca's his coach; he ca's his horse;
He draws a bonie silken purse,
As lang's my tail, whare, thro' the steeks,   *stitches*
The yellow letter'd Geordie keeks.   *guinea peeps*

100

Frae morn to e'en it's nought but toiling,
At baking, roasting, frying, boiling;
An' tho' the gentry first are stechin,   stuffing
Yet ev'n the ha' folk fill their   kitchen-people
   pechan   belly
Wi' sauce, ragouts, an' sic like trashtrie,   trash
That's little short o' downright wastrie.   waste
Our whipper-in, wee, blastet   shrivelled-up
   wonner,   wonder
Poor, worthless elf, it eats a dinner,
Better than ony tenant-man
His Honor has in a' the lan':
An' what poor cot-folk pit their   cottagers
   painch in,   stomach
I own it's past my comprehension.

LUATH

Trowth, Caesar, whyles they're fash't   In truth –
   eneugh: sometimes – troubled
A cotter howkin in a sheugh,   digging – ditch
Wi' dirty stanes biggin a dyke,   building – wall
Baring a quarry, an' sic like;
Himsel, a wife, he thus sustains,
A smytrie o' wee duddie   litter, family –
   weans,   little ragged children
An' nought but his han'-daurg,   hand's labour
   to keep
Them right an' tight in thack an' raep.

An' when they meet wi' sair disasters,
Like loss o' health or want o' masters,
Ye maist wad think, a wee touch langer,   almost
An' they maun starve o' cauld and hunger:
But how it comes, I never kent yet,   knew
They're maistly wonderfu' contented;
An' buirdly chiels, an' clever   stalwart men
   hizzies,   women
Are bred in sic a way as this is.

CAESAR

But then to see how ye're neglecket,
How huff'd, an' cuff'd, an' disrespecket!
L – d man, our gentry care as little
For delvers, ditchers, an' sic cattle;
They gang as saucy by poor folk,
As I wad by a stinking brock.   badge

I've notic'd, on our laird's court-day, –
An' mony a time my heart's been wae, –   sad
Poor tenant bodies, scant o' cash,
How they maun thole a factor's   must endure
   snash;   abuse
He'll stamp an' threaten, curse an' swear
He'll apprehend them, poind   make execution on
   their gear;   goods
While they maun stan', wi' aspect humble,
An' hear it a', an' fear an' tremble!

I see how folk live that hae riches;
But surely poor-folk maun be   must
   wretches!   wretched creatures

LUATH

They're no sae wretched's ane wad think.
Tho' constantly on poortith's brink,   poverty
They're sae accustom'd wi' the sight,
The view o' 't gies them little fright.

Then chance and fortune are sae guided,
They're ay in less or mair provided;
An' tho' fatigu'd wi' close employment,
A blink o' rest's a sweet enjoyment.
The dearest comfort o' their lives,
Their grushie weans an' faithfu'   thriving children
   wives;

The prattling things are just their pride,
That sweetens a' their fire-side.
An' whyles twalpennie worth o' nappy   ale
Can mak the bodies unco happy: very
They lay aside their private cares,
To mind the Kirk and State affairs;
They'll talk o' patronage an' priests,
Wi' kindling fury i' their breasts,
Or tell what new taxation's comin,
An' ferlie at the folk in Lon'on.   wonder

As bleak-fac'd Hallowmass returns,
They get the jovial, rantin
    kirns,   harvest-home rejoicings
When rural life, of ev'ry station,
Unite in common recreation;
Love blinks, Wit slaps, an' social Mirth   shines forth
Forgets there's Care upo' the earth.

That merry day the year begins,
They bar the door on frosty win's;
The nappy reeks wi' mantling   ale smokes
    ream,   froth
An' sheds a heart-inspiring steam;
The luntin pipe, an' sneeshin   puffing out smoke –
    mill,   snuff-box
Are handed round wi' right guid will;
The cantie auld folks cracking   cheery –
    crouse,   talking briskly
The young anes ranting thro' the house – frolicking
My heart has been sae fain to see them,
That I for joy hae barket wi' them.

Still it's owre true that ye hae said   *too*
Sic game is now owre aften play'd;
There's mony a creditable stock
O' decent, honest, fawsont folk,   *seemly*
Are riven out baith root an' branch,   *torn*
Some rascal's pridefu' greed to quench,
Wha thinks to knit himsel the faster
In favour wi' some gentle master,
Wha, aiblins thrang a   *perhaps busy*
   parliamentin',   *in Parliament*
For Britain's guid his saul indentin' –   *good*

CAESAR

Haith, lad, ye little ken about it: *Faith – know little*
For Britain's guid! guid faith! I doubt it.
Say rather, gaun as Premiers lead him: *going*
An' saying aye or no 's they bid him:
At operas an' plays parading,
Mortgaging, gambling, masquerading:
Or maybe, in a frolic daft,   *mad*
To Hague or Calais takes a waft,
To make a tour an' tak a whirl,
To learn *bon ton*, an' see the worl'.

There, at Vienna or Versailles,
He rives his father's auld entails;
Or by Madrid he takes the rout,   *road*
To thrum guitars an' fecht wi' nowt;   *fight – bullocks*
Or down Italian vista startles,
Wh–re-hunting amang groves o' myrtles:
Then bowses drumlie   *drinks –*
   German-water   *turbid mineral-water*
To mak himsel look fair an' fatter,
An' clear the consequential sorrows,
Love-gifts of Carnival signoras.

For Britain's guid! for her destruction!
Wi' dissipation, feud an' faction.

LUATH

Hech man! dear sirs! is that the gate	style
They waste sae mony a braw estate!	many a fine
Are we sae foughten an' harass'd	troubled
For gear to gang that gate at last?	wealth – road

O would they stay aback frae courts,	away from

An' please themsels wi' countra sports,
It wad for ev'ry ane be better,
The laird, the tenant, an' the cotter!

For thae frank, rantin', ramblin' billies,	
Fient haet o' them 's ill-hearted follows;	Not a bit
Except for breakin o' their	cutting down
timmer,	their timber
Or speakin lightly o' their limmer,	mistress

Or shootin o' a hare or moor-cock,
The ne'er-a-bit they're ill to poor folk.

But will ye tell me, master Caesar,
Sure great folk's life's a life o' pleasure?

Nae cauld nor hunger e'er can steer them,	bother

The vera though o' 't need na fear them.

CAESAR

L–d, man, were ye but whyles where I am,
The gentles, ye wad ne'er envy them!
It's true, they need na starve or sweat,

Thro' winter's cauld, or simmer's	cold – summer
heat;	
They've nae sair-wark to craze their	hard work
banes,	
An' fill auld-age wi' grips an' granes:	groans

But human bodies are sic fools,
For a' their colleges an' schools,

That when nae real ills perplex them,	
They mak enow themsels to vex them;	enough
An' ay the less they hae to sturt them,	trouble

In like proportion, less will hurt them.

A country fellow at the pleugh,
His acre's till'd, he's right eneugh;
A country girl at her wheel,
Her dizzen's done, she's unco weel;
But gentlemen, an' ladies warst,   worst
Wi' ev'n-down want o' wark are curst.   work
They loiter, lounging, lank an' lazy;
Tho' deil-haet ails them, yet uneasy;   nothing
Their days insipid, dull an' tasteless;
Their nights unquiet, lang an' restless.

An' ev'n their sports, their balls an' races.
Their galloping through public places,
There's sic parade, sic pomp an' art,
The joy can scarcely reach the heart.

The men cast out in party-matches,
Then sowther a' in deep debauches.   reconcile
Ae night they're mad wi' drink an' wh-ring   One
Niest day their life is past enduring.   Next
The ladies arm-in-arm in clusters,
As great an' gracious a' as sisters;
But hear their absent thoughts o' ither,   each other
They're a' run deils an' jads   downright devils
    thegither.   and wicked women
Whyles, owre the wee bit   Sometimes, over the small
    cup an' platie,   cup of tea
They sip the scandal-potion pretty;
Or lee-lang nights, wi' crabbet leuks, livelong – sour
Pore owre the devil's pictur'd beuks;   cards
Stake on a chance a farmer's stackyard,
An' cheat like onie unhang'd blackguard.   any

There's some exception, man an' woman;
But this is Gentry's life in common.

By this, the sun was out o' sight,
An' darker gloaming brought the night: twilight
The bum-clock humm'd wi' laxy drone;   beetle
The kye stood rowtin i' the loan;   cows – lowing
When up they gat, and shook their lugs, got – rose
Rejoic'd they were na *men*, but *dogs*;
An' each took aff his several way,
Resolv'd to meet some ither day.

To a Mouse

The proverb: 'the best-laid schemes o' mice an' men gang aft a-gley' originates from this poem. Burns's intimate speech to the mouse he has just inadvertently turned out of its house is tender and sympathetic without being sentimental. Both fellow sufferers in an arbitrary world, the mouse's plight is the poet's plight, although for Burns man's burden also included the added dimension of disillusionment and anxiety.

The poem stems from an incident in November 1785, when Burns did plough up a mouse's nest and just succeeded in stopping John Blane, the boy driving the horses, from killing the creature. In this, one of his finest works, he has so beautifully caught a moment of fellowship between two creatures, both of whom have felt pain and fear and the bond between them is greater because of the experience.

To a Mouse

ON TURNING HER UP IN HER NEST, WITH THE PLOUGH,
NOVEMBER 1785

Wee, sleekit, cowrin, tim'rous beastie,	sleek
O, what a panic's in thy breastie!	
Thou need na start awa sae hasty,	
Wi' bickering brattle!	hasty scamper
I wad be laith to rin an' chase thee,	loath
Wi' murd'ring pattle!	

I'm truly sorry Man's dominion
Has broken Nature's social union,
An' justifies that ill opinion,
Which makes thee startle,
At me, thy poor, earth-born companion,
An' fellow-mortal!

I doubt na, whyles, but thou may   sometimes
   thieve;
What then? poor beastie, thou maun live!
A daimen icker in a thrave
'S a sma' request:
I'll get a blessin wi' the lave,   remainder
And never miss't!

Thy wee bit housie, too, in ruin!
Its silly wa's the win's are strewin!
An' naething, now, to big a new ane,   erect
O' foggage green!   moss
An' bleak December's winds ensuin,
Baith snell and keen!   biting

Thou saw the fields laid bare an' waste,
An' weary Winter comin fast,
An' cozie here, beneath the blast,   comfortable
Thou thought to dwell,
Till crash! the cruel coulter past
Out thro' thy cell.

That wee bit heap o' leaves an' stibble,   stubble
Has cost thee mony a weary nibble!
Now thou's turn'd out, for a' thy trouble,
But house or hald,   Without – holding
To thole the Winter's sleety dribble, endure – drizzle
An' cranreuch cauld!   hoar-frost

But Mousie, thou art no thy lane,   not alone
In proving foresight may be vain:
The best-laid schemes o' Mice an' Men
Gang aft a-gley,   go often wrong
An' lea'e us nought but grief and pain, leave
For promis'd joy.

Still thou art blest, compar'd wi' me!
The present only toucheth thee:
But, Och! I backward cast my e'e,
On prospects drear!
An' forward, tho' I canna see,
I guess an' fear!

To Dr Blacklock

Originally from Annan in Dumfriesshire, Dr Thomas Blacklock made a living in Edinburgh teaching, writing poetry and renting out some of his rooms to students. Although blinded in infancy by smallpox he went on to Edinburgh University to read Theology, but after a brief spell as minister at Kirkcudbright Parish Church, he reluctantly realized that he could not perform all his necessary duties.

Returning to Edinburgh he became a well-known and influential figure in the literary world and it was his enthusiastic seal of approval on the Kilmarnock edition of Burns's work that ensured the Ayrshire poet of a welcome in the capital. Burns described Dr Blacklock after their first meeting as 'what I would have expected in our friend, a clear head and an excellent heart'. They remained close after Burns left Edinburgh for Dumfriesshire, until Dr Blacklock's death in 1791. These two rhyming letters were written after a letter by Burns to Blacklock had failed to arrive. Sent by hand with a young minister Robert Heron, but never delivered, the messenger, as Burns suggests, was perhaps waylayed.

To Mr Robert Burns

Edinburgh, 24 August 1789

Dear Burns, thou brother of my heart,
Both for thy virtues and thy art;
If art is may be called in thee,
Which Nature's bounty large and free
With pleasure in thy breast diffuses,
And warms thy soul with all the Muses.
Whether to laugh with easy grace
Thy numbers move the sage's face,
Or bid the softer passions rise,
And ruthless souls with grief surprise,
'Tis Nature's voice distinctly felt,
Through thee, her organ, thus to melt.

Most anxiously I wish to know,
With thee of late how matters go:
How keeps thy much-loved Jean her health?
What promises thy farm of wealth?
Whether the Muse persists to smile,
And all thy anxious cares beguile?
Whether bright fancy keeps alive?
And how thy darling infants thrive?

For me, with grief and sickness spent,
Since I my homeward journey bent,
Spirits depressed no more I mourn,
But vigour, life, and health return.
No more to gloomy thoughts a prey,
I sleep all night and live all day;
By turns my friend and book enjoy,
And thus my circling hours employ;
Happy while yet these hours remain,
If Burns could join the cheerful train,
With wonted zeal, sincere and fervent,
Salute once more his humble servant,

THOMAS BLACKLOCK

To Dr Blacklock

Ellisland, 21 October 1789

Wow, but your letter made me vauntie!	elated
And are ye hale, and weel,	in good health
and cantie?	merry
I ken'd it still your wee bit jauntie	jaunt
Wad bring ye to:	
Lord send you ay as weel 's I want ye,	
And then ye'll do!	

The ill-thief blaw the Heron south!	devil
And never drink be near his drouth!	thirst
He tauld mysel, by word o' mouth,	
He'd tak my letter;	
I lippen'd to the chiel in trouth,	trusted – fellow
And bade nae better	desired

But, aiblins, honest Master Heron	perhaps
Had, at the time, some dainty fair one	
To ware his theologic care on	spend
And holy study;	
And tired o' sauls to waste his lear on,	learning
E'en tried the body.	

But what d'ye think, my trusty fier?	friend
I'm turn'd a gauger – Peace be here!	
Parnassian queens, I fear, I fear	
Ye'll now disdain me,	
And then my fifty pounds a year	
Will little gain me!	

Ye glaiket, gleesome, dainty damies	giddy
Wha, by Castalia's wimplin' streamies,	winding
Lowp, sing, and lave your pretty limbies,	Jump
Ye ken, ye ken	know
That strang necessity supreme is	
'Mang sons o' men.	

I hae a wife and twa wee laddies –
They maun hae brose and   hasty pudding
   brats o' duddies: suits of clothes
Ye ken yoursels my heart right proud is –
I need na vaunt –
But I'll sned besoms – thraw   cut – twist –
   saught woodies,   willow witches
Before they want.

Lord help me thro' this warld o' care!
I'm weary sick o 't late and air!   early
Not but I hae a richer share
Than mony ithers;
But why should ae man better fare,
And a' men brithers?

Come, Firm Resolve, take thou the van,
Thou stalk o' carl-hemp in man!
And let us mind faint heart ne'er wan   won
A lady fair:
Wha does the utmost that he can,
Will whyles do mair.   sometimes – more

But to conclude my silly rhyme
(I'm scant o' verse and scant o' time)
To make a happy fire-side clime
To weans and wife –   children
That's the true pathos and sublime
Of human life.

My compliments to sister Beckie;
And eke the same to honest Lucky:
I wat she is a daintie chuckie
As e'er tread clay;
And gratefully, my gude auld cockie,
I'm yours for ay.

ROBERT BURNS

Willie brew'd a Peck o' Maut

This riotous drinking song was produced in September 1787, through a combined effort, with Burns writing the lyrics and Allan Masterton providing the tune. It is a tribute to a hilarious evening spent near Moffat, when they descended on an unsuspecting William Nicol. Apart from the great sense of happy abandonment, Burns captures so aptly the state of mind of the drunk, who insists he is not drunk, whilst his speech proves the opposite.

Willie brew'd a Peck o' Maut

O Willie brew'd a peck o' maut,   malt
And Rob and Allan cam to pree;   taste
Three blyther hearts, that lee-lang night,   livelong
Ye wad na found in Christendie.

Chorus – We are na fou, we're nae that
       fou,   full [drunk]
       But just a drappie on our e'e   drop – eye
       The cock may craw, the day may
         daw,   dawn
       And ay we'll taste the barley
         bree.   brew, juice

Here are we met, three merry boys,
Three merry boys, I trow, are we;
And mony a night we've merry been,
And mony mae we hope to be!   more

It is the moon, I ken her horn,
That's blinkin' in the lift sae hie;   heavens – high
She shines sae bright to wyle us hame,   lure
But, by my sooth, she'll wait a wee!   a while

Wha first shall rise to gang awa,
A cuckold, coward loun is he!   fellow
Wha last beside his chair shall fa',
He is the King amang us three!

Willie Wastle

The origins of this song are unknown, although it was thought for some time that the role model for Willie was a farmer near Ellisland, who enjoyed the luxury of an ugly, nagging wife. The caricature of Willie's 'dour and din' spouse might seem harsh and excessive today, but she is just an older version of the grotesque, bullying wife, who forms the butt of so many music-hall jokes.

The song was written around 1792 during Burns's later years in Dumfries.

Willie Wastle

TUNE – *The Eight Men of Moidart*

Willie Wastle dwalt on Tweed,
The spot they ca'd it Linkumdoddie;
Willie was a wabster gude   weaver
Cou'd stown a clue wi' ony bodie;
He had a wife was dour and din,   sulky – ill-coloured
O, Tinkler Maidgie was her mither:
Sic a wife as Willie had –
I wad na gie a button for her!

She has an e'e, she has but ane,
The cat has twa the very colour;
Five rusty teeth forbye a stump,   besides
A clapper tongue wad deave a miller;   deafen
A whiskin beard about her mou,   mouth
Her nose and chin they threaten ither: one another
Sic a wife as Willie had –
I wad na gie a button for her!

She's bow-hough'd, she's hem-shin'd bandy-legged
Ae limpin leg a hand-breed
    shorter;   One – hand-breath
She's twisted right, she's twisted left,
To balance fair in ilka quarter   every
She has a hump upon her breast,
The twin o' that upon her shouther:
Sic a wife as Willie had –
I wad na gie a button for her!

Auld baudrons by the ingle sits,   cat – fireside
An' wi' her loof her face a-washin;   paw
But Willie's wife is nae sae trig: dainty
She dights her grunzie wi' a hushion; wipes – mouth
Her walie nieves like-midden-   huge fists – manure
    creels,   panniers
Her face wad fyle the Logan Water: pollute
Sic a wife as Willie had –
I wad na gie a button for her!

The Burns Supper

The Burns Supper

The Burns Supper is celebrated every year on
25 January, the anniversary of the poet's birthday.
Burns Clubs all over the world look forward to this
annual ritual. The evening consists of the tradi-
tional haggis dinner, a helping of Burns's more
famous poems and songs such as 'Tam o' Shanter',
'Holy Willie's Prayer', 'A Red, Red Rose', the
speeches, both serious and funny, and is rounded
off with the singing of 'Auld Lang Syne'.

Before the dinner begins 'The Selkirk Grace' is
said as Burns rendered it at the home of the Earl of
Selkirk at St Mary's Isle, Kirkcudbright. After the
first course is served the chairman for the evening
asks the company to stand for the arrival of the
haggis. A piper leads the procession, followed by
the chef carrying the haggis on a platter and lastly a
third person carrying two bottles of whisky. The
assembled company gives a slow handclap as it
makes its way to the top table. The chairman or
one of the guests then recites Burns's address 'To
a Haggis' (composed around 1786), and as he
comes to the line 'An' cut you up wi' ready sleight',
he slits open the haggis with a knife.

To a Haggis

Fair fa' your honest, sonsie face,	good luck to – jolly
Great Chieftain o' the Puddin-race!	
Aboon them a' ye tak your place,	above
Painch, tripe or thairm:	paunch – intestines
Weel are ye wordy o' a grace	worthy
As lang's my arm.	

The groaning trencher there ye fill,	
Your hurdies like a distant hill	buttocks
Your pin wad help to mend a mill	would
In time o' need,	
While thro' your pores the dews distil	
Like amber bead.	

His knife see Rustic-labour dight,   clean, wipe
An' cut you up wi' ready sleight,
Trenching your gushing entrails bright
Like onie ditch;   any
And then, O what a glorious sight,
Warm-reekin, rich!   steaming

Then, horn for horn they stretch an'
   strive,   horn – spoon
Deil tak the hindmost, on they drive,   last
Till a' their weel-swall'd kytes   swelled stomachs
   belyve   by and by
Are bent like drums;
Then auld Guidman, maist like to rive almost – burst
  'Bethankit' hums.   murmurs 'God be thanked'

Is there that owre his French *ragout*,   over
Or *olio* that wad staw a sow,   would surfeit
Or *fricassee* wad mak her spew
Wi' perfect sconner,   disgust
Looks down wi' sneering, scornfu' view
On sic a dinner?   such

Poor devil! see him owre his trash,
As feckless as a wither'd rash,   feeble – rush
His spindle shank a guid whip-lash,   thin leg – good
His nieve a nit;   closed fist – nut
Thro' bluidy flood or field to dash,   bloody
O how unfit!

But mark the Rustic, haggis-fed,
The trembling earth resound his tread;
Clap in his walie nieve a blade,   large fist
He'll make it whissle;   whistle
An' legs, an' arms, an' heads will sned   lop off
Like taps o' thrissle.   tops of thistles

Ye Pow'rs wha mak mankind your care
And dish them out their bill o' fare,
Auld Scotland wants nae skinking ware   thin stuff
That jaups in luggies;   splashes in bowls
But if ye wish her gratefu' prayer,
Gie her a Haggis!   give

The address finished, the piper and chef are given a dram of the whisky and everyone drinks a toast to the haggis. Haggis is traditionally made from the heart, lights and liver of a sheep. After parboiling, these parts are minced and suet, onion, oatmeal and seasonings are added. The mixture is sewn up in the stomach bag of a sheep and boiled for four to five hours. It is usually served with mashed turnip and potato.

After dinner the speeches begin. The major speech of the evening is the 'Immortal Memory', which normally lasts about half an hour. The speaker's task is to illuminate Robert Burns's achievements and his contribution to Scotland. Sometimes a particular facet of his life is examined, whether his rigorous early days, his time in Edinburgh or the end of his life in Dumfries. The speaker might prefer to consider what Burns's attitudes to life today might be or to reflect on some of the qualities which made the man and the poet. The purpose behind the speech is to encourage the listener to read Burns, to think about what he said about his life and dwell on his reasons for saying it.

The 'Appreciation of the Immortal Memory' follows and is a short thank you to the speaker for his thoughts and insights.

The 'Toast to the Lassies' is the first of two witty speeches in which the men and woman alternately lambast one another with their different defects and attributes. This first toast should be a witty, fun-packed look at the 'fairer sex', as Burns saw them and as they are seen today, from the ugly, nagging wife in 'Willie Wastle' to the temptress Clarinda. It should end on a warm, affectionate note, praising the lassies, as Burns surely would, whereupon the men rise and drink the toast to them.

The 'Response' is the ladies' chance to retaliate by sighting men's foibles and weaknesses and pointing out their own superiority and fidelity. Burns can be used to back this up by quoting these lines from 'Green grow the Rashes':

Auld Nature swears, the lovely dears
Her noblest work she classes, O:
Her prentice han' she try'd on man,
An' then she made the lasses, O.

Like the speech before this should end on a happy, conciliatory note.

These are the traditional speeches which are a must at a Burns Supper, but others can be added and it must be remembered that the poems, songs and whisky which intersperse the evening are a vital component of the event.

In conclusion the festivities are brought to a close with everyone singing 'Auld Lang Syne'.

Bibliography

Chambers, Robert, *The Life and Works of Robert Burns,* Vols I–IV, Chambers, Edinburgh, 1896

Crawford, Thomas, *Burns: A Study of the Poems and Songs,* Oliver and Boyd, Edinburgh, 1960

Daiches, David, *Robert Burns and His World,* Thames and Hudson, London, 1971

De Lancey Ferguson, J. (ed), *The Letters of Robert Burns,* Vols 1–11, Oxford University Press, Oxford, 1931

De Lancey Ferguson, J., *Pride and Passion,* Oxford University Press, Oxford, 1939

Jack, Ronald D.S. and Andrew Noble (eds), *The Art of Robert Burns,* Vision Press, London, 1982

Keith, Christina, *The Russet Coat,* Robert Hale, London, 1956

Snyder, Franklyn Bliss, *The Life of Robert Burns,* Macmillan, London, 1932

Also published by Chambers

Wallace, William (ed), *Poetical Works of Robert Burns,* Chambers, Edinburgh, 1990

Index of First Lines

A guid New-year I wish thee, Maggie!	70
Ae fond kiss, and then we sever	27
But warily tent, when ye come to court me	59
Coming through the rye, poor body	36
Fair fa' your honest, sonsie face	119
Flow gently, sweet Afton, among thy green braes	29
Go, fetch to me a pint o' wine	57
Here Stewarts once in glory reigned	52
Is there for honest Poverty	45
It was upon a Lammas night	96
John Anderson, my jo, John	51
Lament in rhyme, lament in prose	60
My lov'd, my honor'd, much respected friend!	77
O my Luve's like a red, red rose	31
O Thou that in the heavens does dwell!	47
O Thou! whatever title suit thee	19
O Willie brew'd a peck o' maut	113
O ye wha are sae guid yoursel	24
Scots, wha hae wi' Wallace bled	35
Should auld acquaintance be forgot	33
Some books are lies frae end to end	38
Some hae meat and canna eat	97
The deil cam fiddling thro' the town	84
The last time I came o'er the moor	94
There was three kings into the east	53
'Twas in that place o' Scotland's isle	99
Upon a simmer Sunday morn	86
Wee, sleekit, cowrin, tim'rous beastie	107
When chapman billies leave the street	63
Willie Wastle dwalt on Tweed	115
Wow, but your letter made me vauntie!	111
Ye banks and braes o' bonie Doon	75

A Man's a Man for a' that

Is there for honest Poverty
That hings his head, and a' that?   all that
The coward-slave, we pass him by,
We dare be poor for a' that!
For a' that, and a' that,
Our toils obscure, and a' that,
The rank is but the guinea's stamp,
The Man's the gowd for a' that!

What though on hamely fare we dine,
Wear hoddin grey, and a' that;   coarse cloth
Gie fools their silks and knaves their wine,
A Man's a Man for a' that:
For a' that, and a' that,
Their tinsel show, and a' that;
The honest man, tho' e'er sae poor,
Is king o' men for a' that!

Ye see yon birkie ca'd a lord   fellow
Wha struts, and stares, and a' that,
Though hundreds worship at his word,
He's but a coof for a' that: fool, ninny
For a' that, and a' that,
His ribband, star and a' that;
The man of independent mind
He looks and laughs at a' that.

A prince can mak a belted knight,
A marquis, duke and a' that;
But an honest man's aboon his might —   above
Gude faith, he mauna fa' that!   must not
For a' that, and a' that,
Their dignities, and a' that;
The pith o' sense and pride o' worth
Are higher rank than a' that.

Then let us pray that come it may, —
As come it will for a' that —
That Sense and Worth, o'er a' the earth,
May bear the gree, and a' that.   supremacy
For a' that, and a' that,
It's comin' yet for a' that,
That Man to Man, the world o'er,
Shall brothers be for a' that!

45

Holy Willie's Prayer

Burns's glorious hypocrite 'Holy Willie' is still instantly recognizable today. With wonderful irony, he delivers a lash upon his own back in every line. One of Burns's finest pieces of work, it was written in the summer of 1785 when his landlord and friend Gavin Hamilton was finally absolved by higher Church courts of not keeping the Sabbath. The chief instigator of the prosecution was William Fisher, a Church elder and member of the Kirk Session of Mauchline Parish Church, which first 'tried' Hamilton for such crimes as picking potatoes on Sunday and not attending Church. A Mauchline man by birth, Hamilton lived there with his wife and young family, practising as a lawyer and administering the poor fund. A kind-hearted and generous friend to many, he was the very antitheses of William Fisher.

Fisher, born the son of a farmer in 1737, became an elder of Mauchline Church in 1772. A gossiping, smug, zealous upholder of strict Calvinist tenets, he came unstuck in 1790, when he was